*"I was one of the first benef
families under the umbrella (
This group changed my life fr
the great loss of a parent to a young ...
a brighter future. The GoGo Trust led by Sharron
Frood became like stars guiding us into hope.
I learned great lessons against a backlash of grief
and abandonment. Today, I am a businessman
and a man of determination and character."*
Mr Luyanda Fitoli

*"This book is beautiful and thoughtful. It's our story. It is
about hope not only for South Africa but also for Africa.
I am proud to lead this work."*
Mr Mtutuzeli Beyi,
GoGo Trust Co-ordinator Kwazakhele

"A compelling and captivating story."
Rev Jean Underwood,
Former Director of the House of Resurrection Haven

*"I love this book. It is written with love and humility. Dr
Frood offers an inspiring testament to the resilience of
the human spirit, weaving together powerful stories of
overcoming poverty and hardship with hope. She calls us
to support and uplift those in need through faith in
action."*
Dr Margaret Williams,
Associate Professor, Nelson Mandela University

"This isn't so much a book as it is like having a conversation with Sharron over coffee. I've been fortunate to have been to and seen first-hand some of the places and met some of the people Sharron writes about, and I thank her for the authenticity of each word. You can't read this book without being impacted by the hope and humanity that come off every page. As a broadcast industry professional, I've seen plenty of times when the hype and drama surrounding a story are bigger than the actual story itself. Where the people at the centre get lost in the documenting and storytelling, this is the opposite. This book tells a simple, matter-of-fact story of lives changed and futures transformed in a way that makes it accessible and has the main characters as the main characters."
Mr Rory Springthorpe,
Founder and CEO, Vivid Broadcasting

"I met Sharron when she was a University of Port Elizabeth Honours student. Her gentle demeanour belied the depth of what she had embarked on in our city. The focal point of her narrative reveals God's heart towards widows and orphans. Sharron beautifully demonstrates true discipleship as her story unfolds over two decades, culminating in sustainable Indigenous leadership in the structures she establishes. The story, told with authentic vulnerability, invites the reader to cultivate greater obedience to God's will, irrespective of its inconvenience. Inevitably, Sharron's story stirs a desire to care for vulnerable people. As the Vice-Chancellor capped Sharron at her doctoral graduation, a resounding roar erupted from a cluster of GoGos, causing the VC to stop and ask her who they were. Their applause honoured a stranger who had come into their midst to live in their hearts. Her love restored hope in an African township."
Dr Ruth Connelly,
Counselling Psychologist

"Sharron's intimate story will inspire you. It's honest and real. Deep heartache and extreme suffering in the wake of the HIV tragedy in South Africa still speak hope, though, because, through his believers, Jesus cares."
**Dr John Scholtz, Retired Senior Pastor,
Harvest Christian Church, Port Elizabeth, South Africa**

"This book is not merely about a social upliftment project in a township in South Africa. It's not just a collection of stories about lives ravaged by HIV or poverty. It is a rather detailed and inspiring record of the tangible power of a Heavenly Father who chooses to redeem and transform lives through his word and goodness."
**Rev Keith du Plessis,
Member, Apostolic Council; Church of the Nations**

"Sharron stands out for her genuine dedication to others, providing lasting solutions for the underprivileged. She sows seeds of change, impacting future generations and active participants as doers, not just a hearer."
**Mr Bongani Njamini,
Chartered Accountant and GoGo Board of Trustees Member**

"Julian's Children have supported my sister and me for over eight years. I am working and studying to become a businessman. I am planning to open a restaurant in Kwazakhele."
**Mr Ayabonga Beyi,
Supported by Julian's Children.**

"The GoGo Trust has done remarkable work in our community. We love Sharron, and she loves us."
Mama Mandisa

YELLOW
THE COLOUR OF
HOPE

Copyright © 2024 Sharron Frood

The moral right of the author has been asserted.

Apart from any fair dealing for the purposes of research or private study, or criticism or review, as permitted under Copyright, Design and Patents Act 1998, this publication may only be reproduced, stored or transmitted, in any form or by any means, with prior permission in writing of the publishers, or in any case of the reprographic reproduction in accordance with the terms of licences issued by the Copyright Licensing Agency. Enquiries concerning reproduction outside these terms should be sent to the publishers.

PublishU Ltd

www.PublishU.com

Scripture from the Holy Bible, New International Version®, NIV®. Copyright © 1973, 1978, 1984, 2011 by Biblica, Inc.™ Used by permission of Zondervan. All rights reserved worldwide.

Quotes taken from The Case for a Creator by Lee Strobel. Copyright © 2004 by Lee Strobel. Used by permission of HarperCollins Christian Publishing.

All rights of this publication are reserved.

Thanks

I want to thank my friend's daughter, Peace, for her constant encouragement, support, and words, "Don't you need to go and write Sharron?" Thank you for believing, praying, and understanding when I needed to shut myself away to write.

Thank you to Sam Stevens, who undertook the Publish U writing course two years before me and encouraged me into the space where I can work full-time and write a book. I am grateful for your example.

To my friends who have cheered me along the way, I am grateful for you all and appreciate your accompaniment on this journey. Thank you to Sam, Catrina, Mel, Robyn, Chenise, Min, Jade, Philippa and Ruth.

To Mtutuzeli and Lulama, thank you for believing and for your suggestions. This is our story, and I am glad that you like it.

To the GoGo Trust board of trustees, thank you for encouraging me to write this book. I am thankful for your support and all you do to make this work possible.

Thank you to Dr Jacquie Collin, Sandie Reeves, Philippa O'Brien and Sarah White for editing my first draft. Your thoughtful, informed, wise, and comprehensive comments have made this book better. I hope you are encouraged to see the changes you advised written on the pages of this version.

To Mr Matt Bird, "Yes, I can" is what I learned from you. Thank you for being the very essence of true encouragement.

To my family, thank you for letting me go to undertake this work even when you didn't understand and it was costly for you to let me go. You supported and visited me; for that, I am genuinely grateful. I hope that you are inspired and encouraged.

To the Mamas and Children, you are remarkable. Thank you for letting us hear the cry of your hearts and for opening up your homes and your lives to me. I remain inspired by you and am honoured to know you all. Your lives speak; remember Indemiso (Psalm 23).

To all those who financially support the work of the GoGo Trust, your kind, generous, faithful giving has made this possible. This story also belongs to you. It does take a village to raise a child.

Contents

Chapter 1 Discovering Endless Hope

Chapter 2 The Yes Becomes a Go

Chapter 3 Tuesdays Became Wednesdays and Thursdays...

Chapter 4 Being Seen

Chapter 5 Visiting

Chapter 6 Children Become Orphans. They Are Not Born Orphans

Chapter 7 Pulling Together What Was Said

Chapter 8 Sisonke Sophumelela and Julian's Children

Chapter 9 A Remarkable Man

Chapter 10 Sewing Machines

Chapter 11 Julian's Children

Chapter 12 Creating Hopeful Solutions

Conclusion I Leave You With This: A Poem

References

About the Author

About the Organisation

Foreword

Imagine your life this way:

Hope (not her real name) is 14 years old and lives in Kwazakhele townships in Gqeberha (formally Port Elizabeth) in the Eastern Cape Province of South Africa.

She lives in a shack, an informal dwelling in the middle of Kwazakhele, that is without running water and is often hungry. It's dusty. The shack that is her home is made from corrugated iron and some wood and is fastened together in an ad-hoc manner. It's like an oven in the summer and a fridge in the winter. The earth outside her home is hard after being baked in the sun. Nothing grows except weeds and the occasional resilient plant, and the vegetables are carefully planted in a small but well-cared-for vegetable patch behind the shack. There is not much aesthetically pleasing, but much hope is expressed in the smiles of her neighbours, who are respectfully quiet. They accompany her in life with their presence. Dogs are chained to posts, and the chains rattle as the dogs try to wander through the yards of other shacks close by.

Children not yet old enough to go to school play barefoot on the un-tarmacked roads. Their toys are simple and carefully crafted from old tyres, scraps of wire, and old Coca Cola and Fanta cans. Car wheels are made from these cans that are fastened together with wire to make car and truck wheels. Then, the imaginations of the children create adventures for these toys.

The taxis drive quickly nearby, a man shouting "town" "town" out of the window of each taxi, touting for customers as they drive into town. Each taxi is crowded with people, and the drivers play loud music and always honk their horns.

As we drove to visit Hope in Kwazakhele, we went through Njoli Square (a square in the middle of Kwazakhele where all the roads merge at a roundabout or traffic circle). On the corner of this square, I saw live chickens being sold in supermarket shopping trolleys. Sheep's heads were also being cooked on open wooden fires. Floodlights stood tall in the blue sky, lighting the townships at night. Grey steel security point lookouts were also seen in the sky, a reminder of the apartheid era.

I was accompanied by Mr Nikelo, a community member, on this visit to Hope's home. Before driving to her house, he advised me on gifts to take and what to wear. I was told to dress down but to wear a skirt. We took rice, beans, cooking oil, onions, oranges, soap, biscuits, juice, Panardo (paracetamol), and bread with us.

The sky was very blue, a beautiful blue, different to the sky in England. The rubbish was everywhere, blown by the unrelenting wind, which was unpleasant and full of dust. I will try to describe the smell. Residents in informal settlements don't have flushing toilets. Toilets are buckets collected weekly by the municipality and replaced with clean ones. These buckets are housed in smaller single shacks separate from the main shack where people live. A seat for this bucket is constructed from wood, and the bucket is placed underneath. This bucket is replaced weekly, but this smell lingers. When the wind blew, this smell dominated every sense. This, combined with heat and dust, made this neighbourhood a challenging place to live.

Poverty was everywhere, offending every sense. Yet, in the middle of this, I met Hope. She greeted us with a smile as we walked to her front door. She was wearing flip flops and a tee shirt, which was clean and un-ironed. She wore a red skirt that fitted her, and her hair was clean and brushed back into a bun. The windows of her home were opened. I noticed her house was inviting and spotless in the middle of her surroundings. She was welcoming but shy and knew Mr Nikelo, whom she greeted respectfully.

Hope's brother was at school. She was very proud of him and spoke about his future and her delight in his opportunity to attend school. He would arrive home from school to a meal prepared for him by Hope before he did his homework by candlelight in a quiet corner of their home.

Hope was caring for her mother, who had AIDS. She collected water, cooked meals, cleaned the home, and attended to her mother's needs. This was my first visit to meet a young person who lived in a shack. I saw such dignity and found myself humbled.

Hope spoke to us about the challenges of caring for her mum and her hopes of returning to school one day. She wanted to become a teacher. We read Psalm 23 together and prayed; we left the gifts we had brought and had juice and biscuits together before I left to return to my home in this city. This was my first of many visits to children's homes in Kwazakhele and surrounding township communities in Gqeberha. These townships are home to approximately 750,000 people as of the last census. This book is about visiting widows and orphans in these communities, their remarkable lives and their beautiful, dignified, life-giving faith.

Introduction

When women become widows and children become orphans, they experience complex vulnerability. In the context of the South African Townships, this is magnified due to socio-economic poverty, the legacies of apartheid, and the HIV/AIDS pandemic. In South Africa, the legislative and policy frameworks that guide the South African government's interventions for educating, caring for and supporting children are comprehensive and rich. The roots of this are in international law, predominantly the Convention on the Rights of the Child (1) stewarding the principle of "best Interests", which finds its expression in section 28 of the Bill of Rights in the South African Constitution (2). This intention has been further expressed in the Children Act of 2005 and the National Plan of Action for Children (2019-2024) (3).

This National Plan of Action for Children (3) clearly states what the South African Government intends to do but is ambiguous concerning how to do it. This creates an implementation gap. This gap is filled by many non-governmental organisations (NGOs). As an academic, I have published academic papers concerning how this gap could be closed through implementing comprehensive strategies using a "bottom-up" approach informed by children who have become AIDS orphans and who are living in these communities and by some of the professionals responsible for caring and supporting these vulnerable children. However, this book is not about this; it's about the stories of remarkable women and children living as widows and orphans in township communities in South Africa and their faith in a loving God.

The GoGo Trust is but one NGO filling a gap. The GoGo Trust is a registered Non-Governmental Organisation I founded in April 2003 whilst living and working in South Africa and still oversee. It exists to help and support widows and orphans living in Kwazakhele and surrounding township communities in Gqeberha. GoGo in Xhosa means grandmother. GoGos, however, are remarkable, loving, kind, generous, dignified, purposeful, capable, and generous women. In 2023, the GoGo Trust celebrated its 20th anniversary. It felt a fitting time to write a book to commemorate this.

I cycle to work in London and have done so for many years. When I was growing up, we had cycling proficiency on Fridays at school to learn to ride our bikes safely. We were taught the Green Cross code. We learnt to stop, look and listen. As an aside and as a person who cycles in London, I would be grateful if there was a Green Cross code campaign to encourage us all to stop, look and listen before crossing the road.

These words, Stop, look, and listen, could be helpful when considering visiting widows and orphans. We stop and think about the people we are about to visit; we look and see what we could take to the visit, which could be for their good. When visiting, we take the time to listen to what is being said and what is unsaid by the visitee. Visiting can be complex. It takes time and humility. Visiting requires intentionality, generosity, listening, and humility; it costs us something.

Driving into the Kwazakhele township to visit widows and orphans in Gqeberha taught me a lot. The environment is harsh and unrelenting, with vast challenges always speaking of a lack of worth and hopelessness to the people who live there. Yet there was another narrative to discover: one of dignity, purpose, hope, and a rich, inspiring, life-giving faith expressed in the language of the GoGos and the children I visited and still visit.

I've often been asked why I went to South Africa. When I was writing my PhD., I developed a conceptual framework upon which strategies were developed to be considered for implementation by policymakers in South Africa to improve care and support for these vulnerable children. Essentially, I was writing a thinking map using concepts fully explained as they emerged in the data collected for my PhD. Writing a book is very different.

My faith is deeply personal, and I share the language of my endless hope with those close to me. In writing Yellow, the colour of hope, my endless hope will be visible. This is not unlike developing a conceptual framework using language to explain my heart responding to endless hope, which led me to South Africa. My endless hope has deepened over time, but with an unabating persuasion that guides my life.

I wrote this book to tell some of the stories of the GoGo Trust, and many have said you should write a book, Sharron. Most importantly, Mtutuzeli asked me to.

I also want to commend you to the GoGos, whom I call Mamas, and the children whose stories appear in this book. I wish to commend you to Mtutuzeli and Lulama

Beyi, who are remarkable people. Their faithfulness is exemplary, and their friendship is encouraging.

As you read this book, which I hope encourages you, the work of the Soup Cells and the visiting Julian's Children continues in tandem.

I want to lead with this; "As we move between the dichotomies of life, we feel the pulse of life, a pull homeward. We feel the tension between giving up and going on... Hope is the space between... Between the concrete and the intangible; between evidence and intuition; between religion and spirituality; between faith and doubt" (4).

Chapter 1
Discovering Endless Hope

"Yellow is a colour that cannot be ignored. It is bright, bold, and impossible to miss."
– Author unknown

As I look out of the window of my London flat, I notice the rising sun tinting the sky slightly yellow. The flowers in a vase on the kitchen table are beautiful, and some are a delicate yellow. The candle on my desk as I write this has a yellow flame. We have a guest for breakfast, and I have just been to the shop to buy some croissants. They are golden and inside a lovely yellow.

If this were an academic paper, I would define yellow and justify why I chose it as the name for the title of this book. But as this is not an academic paper but a book, I want to assure you that yellow, the colour of hope, will become apparent by the end of this chapter.

I recently returned home from visiting friends who live near the coast in Northern Ireland. It is beautiful; I would even use the word magnificent. Each morning, my friend would pick me up from where I was staying and drive me to the beach, where she and her friends would swim in the icy water.

I sat on a rock on this beach looking out to sea. While listening to these singing cold-water swimmers, I saw a seal. Was he looking at me, or was it her? It was a still and very fresh morning. I was thinking about the book writing course I would start in the coming weeks and had been thinking about a title for months. This book would be about endless hope, and as I watched the sunrise that morning on the beach, I thought if hope could be a colour for me, it would be yellow. For you, it might be green, blue, or pink. After my friend finished swimming and I returned to the cottage where I stayed, I wrote Yellow the Colour of Hope in my journal.

When I think about yellow, I think of when I was a child growing up sitting in my bedroom, at the kitchen table, or on special occasions at the dining table, colouring in my colouring book. I used to have pencils; you know, the ones where they have lots of colours in them, and you take out and slot in the colour you need. I loved using that pencil to colour in. My colourings always had a streak of yellow in them. I remember sitting on the back lawn, playing with my friends, making daisy chains and holding buttercup flowers under our chins. We would say, "Do you like butter?", it always reflected yellow.

My Granny and Grandad gave me a children's bible as a Christmas gift. Yep, you have it, on the cover; there is a flash of yellow. I remember many happy memories of playing in their garden. Granny would call us in for supper, and we would have jam and cream with a delicate yellow crust on the top. I have always loved walking in the woods in autumn, as the leaves turn different shades of yellow. In winter, I am comforted by the yellow flames flicking in open fires and the candles I light, but most of all, the flash of yellow is beautiful. Yellow can be found in these things and in the flash of yellow in the lovely winter scarf my Mum knitted for me as a gift a few Christmases ago.

My family did not attend church regularly when I was growing up, but I did. I used to be allowed to walk to church if I told Mum and Dad whether I was walking the Top, Middle, or Bottom way; there was so much choice on a Sunday morning. I have always loved going to church. As children, we would go to Sunday school first, walk into church, and sit on our little chairs at the back. The vicar was dressed in a white robe. His face was kind and friendly, just like the man in Grizzly Bear Adams, a TV show we were allowed to watch as a treat on a Sunday afternoon when I was a child.

The vicar used to stand at the brass lectern, behind him a stained-glass window full of yellow. When the sun shone on that window, all the rainbow colours shone into the church like a kaleidoscope. When it was time for holy communion, all the children would go to the altar made of yellowish wood, and the vicar would sign the cross over our heads and say a blessing. This made me feel so safe, especially when the yellow light reflected through the window streaming into the church.

After the hymns were sung, we would walk into the Sunday school building, sit on yellow benches, have a drink and a biscuit, and go to our activity tables. At the end of Sunday school, we would receive a stamp for putting into our stamp book – the kind of stamp on an envelope when you post a letter. I still have my stamp book, and I recently looked through it to find that each of the stamps we received had a splash of yellow. I remember Dad picking me up, and I would go home for a roast dinner. I loved those crispy roast potatoes, which are, of course, primarily yellow. My school uniform at primary school was red, and at secondary school, it was maroon, with a flash of yellow on the badge of my blazer and tie. At primary school, the building was cream; the only yellow outside was in the painted lines on the playground to make the colours of the netball pitch.

I remember going into the assembly hall of this school, where we would sing hymns from our hymnbooks. My favourite hymn was, "Oh Jesus, I have promised to serve thee to the end to be forever near me, my master and my friend. I shall not fear the battle if thou are by my side nor wander from the pathway if thou wilt be my guide". I loved this hymn and used to sing it with all my heart. This room always had some yellow as my teachers hung our school paintings in this assembly hall. I also used to play my recorder at school concerts in this hall. It was black, but its case was yellow, and I loved carrying my recorder to school.

I first went to Africa and visited Zambia with two friends, when I was twenty-three. We assisted pastors Timothy and Bupe, who had previously attended Bible school in the UK. The same Bible school I have also attended. There was a lot of yellow during this time, and the sun brightened everything. We saw miracles and much suffering, too, during this trip. Physically, living was hard, and we slept on the floor on reed mats. I ate termites once and loved eating Cassava and ground nut sauce. This time was rich. If I were to write in one sentence about this time, it would be simple. The Jesus I read about in the bible became the Jesus I saw working in people's lives every day, and scripture came alive to me profoundly. I have been afraid to write this as I fear being misunderstood and judged. I cannot write this book without acknowledging Jesus, my endless hope. If you are reading this and are not feeling yellow, I hope you can be encouraged by this hope. I have found my endless hope.

Two years later, I took my second trip to Africa, this time to Uganda. I loved the yellow bananas, the orange soil, and the light green leaves on the trees. I loved the warm generosity of people and the children I met at Kapeeka Orphanage. My trip to Zambia taught me to believe in miracles, and my trip to Uganda taught me to love people, to go the extra mile and to care for children whose parents had been killed during the Idi Amin regime. The children I met at Kapeeka village were beautiful, full of love and gratitude, and willing to learn. They were so grateful and joyous.

I taught the children at Kapeeka Orphanage primary health care using the child-to-child education program (5). I taught them how to stay healthy in their context and what to do if they became sick. Before the orphanage was established, a minister, Robert Kayanja, found the children of Kapeeka living in the trees. I have read many times in the scripture that "God is father to the fatherless and defender of the widow" (Psalm 68 v5-6).

Seeing with my own eyes children who had been living in the trees now sleeping in beds, going to school, and being kind to me, a stranger, gave me such hope. They listened intently as I taught them in the classroom. One afternoon, they brought a young man with a leg ulcer to me. We cleaned it using boiled salty water and covered it with Mango skin. We hollowed out a mango, put the skin side up, and covered his wound. We cleaned and covered this wound for five days, and it began to improve. I taught the children to do this so that they could continue cleaning and covering wounds once I was gone using what they had available. I brought the child-to-child education book and the books "Where There Is No Doctor" (6) and "Where There Is No Dentist" (7) to leave behind for the headteacher of this school. These gave great tips to help children stay healthy and treat minor illnesses and wounds. There was much yellow at this time in the bananas we ate in the sunshine and in the joy, we were surrounded by in these children's songs.

Writing this, I can see that I learnt to love Africa and African people during these two trips. I loved the beauty and appreciated the rich uniqueness of both. I also learned to embrace and appreciate the miraculous. The scripture "God is father to the fatherless and defender of the widow" was written in my heart. Little did I know then that the seeds of a new beginning had been sown. I had seen love in action and the miraculous.

A few years later, I began working in Kwazakhele Township in Gqeberha (formally Port Elizabeth) in South Africa in April 2002, visiting women who are widows and children who are living as AIDS orphans in this community. Mr. Nikelo, a Kwazakhele health and welfare forum member, invited me into the community. I was a registered student on a Bachelor Curationis honours degree in Advanced Primary Health Care degree at the time at the University of Port Elizabeth (UPE), renamed the Nelson Mandela University (NMU). From this point, I will refer to this university's current name, NMU. Mr. Nikelo was a link person between the Kwazakhele Health and Welfare Forum and this university's faculty of Health Sciences.

Kwazakhele, in the local Xhosa language, means "a place to build yourself". On arriving in Kwazakhele township for the first time with Mr Nikelo, I parked my car where I was directed, and we got out and visited Hope. After this visit, Mr Nikelo and I walked along a path back to my car. I saw a tree, which was unusual as there are few trees in these township communities. At the base of the tree, I saw a flower growing. It was a perfectly formed trumpet, lily. This lily was perfect. The flower was unblemished, the stem was light green, and the middle of this lily was bright yellow. I thought about Hope, whom we had just visited, and how, in the middle of such suffering, we had seen such dignity and love, and now this lily in the middle of the harsh and dusty ground where there was rubbish and dogs and dust, I saw a beautiful flower growing in hard ground. I still have the photograph of this lily. I have seen hope and beauty in a place of feeling overwhelmed and surrounded by poverty. In the middle of this flower, which was perfectly white, was a bright yellow perfectly formed stamen. This is why I have called this book "Yellow, the Colour of Hope".

SHARRON FROOD

Chapter 2
The Yes Becomes a Go

"How lovely Yellow is! It stands for the sun."
– Vincent Van Gogh

Our lives are like trees. We have roots that people cannot see, but the nutrients in those roots become visible in the leaves or fruit on the trees. I will try to explain my roots, that is, the journey of my heart. In other words, I will explain my faith and hope story, which led me to drive my car into a township community in South Africa to visit widows and orphans. This, on one level, is deeply personal, but I hope it is also seen through the work of the GoGo Trust and by those who know me.

The light on my desk casts a soft yellow across the page as I write; it is the only yellow I can see today. No member of my family had ever been to Africa before me. I did not grow up in a home where we spoke about Africa. I did not have friends from Africa, nor did we eat African food. The first African people I met were children I nursed as a student nurse at Great Ormond Street Hospital in London. I felt intrigued by the depth and richness of African culture, and I still do.

Why did I go to South Africa?

The journey of a thousand miles begins with one step, Lao Tzu.

The question I have been asked countless times is, why did you go to South Africa? In short, the journey of my own heart led me to a place where I felt compelled.

Others might call it a calling. My heart had grown in faith, and I was persuaded that I was to go. I wanted to give up many times when I lived in South Africa as I felt continually challenged, but there was always new strength that did not come from me.

My life before Africa.

Growing up in Devon, I have many happy memories of picking primrose, going to the beach, eating fish and chips, and having ice cream. We had a lovely garden of flowers, runner beans, and potatoes. I remember playing outside, riding my bike, and playing football. My Dad used to push my brother and me in the wheelbarrow; somehow, life was simple. I had always wanted to become a nurse.

Becoming a student nurse at Great Ormond Street Children's Hospital in London was exciting, but I started this journey with my brother unwell with leukaemia. I mention this here because it is of significance. During my first week as a student nurse at Great Ormond Street Children's Hospital, we were invited to a small evening event to meet newly-qualified nurses. We were beyond excited as we walked up the stairs of the nurses' home, a group of giggling 19-year-olds. Our conversation was about what we would do when we qualified. I remember someone saying they wanted to work in intensive care, someone else said they wanted to work with children who needed kidney transplants, and another wanted to care for children who had cancer. When asked what I would do after training, I said, "I will be a missionary in Africa"; the words rolled off my tongue. I remember thinking, what is a missionary, and why Africa?

Julian

In December of that year, my brother Julian died of leukaemia. He died two months before his 18th birthday. He was my only sibling. Now, our world was shaken. During this time, my roots grew in a dark place. Six months into my course as a student nurse at Great Ormond Street Hospital in London, I was heartbroken. How would my heart navigate this loss?

My life became about my studies and clinical placements, and I was fortunate to have lovely friends. When he died, I saw his spirit go to heaven. In that moment, eternity touched my life, and heaven became a reality. Then I read scripture daily and found endless hope in the middle of pain, confusion, and, dare I say it, at times, lament. The scriptures that were life and strength for my heart were (Psalm 73 v 26), "My heart and flesh may fail, but God is the strength of my heart and my portion forever". I found this to be true. Day after day there was strength to complete my placements, make new friends, comfort sick children and their families, learn and complete assignments. My faith grew. Scriptures such as "He who dwells in the shelter of the Most High will rest in the shadow of the almighty" (Psalm 91 v1) were life to me. I wanted to rest in the shadow of the Almighty; I felt safe there in a world I struggled to make sense of. My other favourite scripture is (Psalm 34 v 18): "The Lord is close to the broken-hearted and saves those who are crushed in spirit". Then I read the story of Keith Green, written by his wife Melody Green, "A Cry in the Wilderness", and I was able to, in part, identify with some of her experiences relating to loss. The God in the Bible became very real, and I found life in going to church.

During my training to become a Staff nurse, I missed a lot of church due to working long days at weekends. I wanted to study scripture, so a year after qualifying as a nurse, I started Bible school at Roffey Place in Sussex, the same Bible school Bupe and Timothy had attended a few years before.

"Once you choose hope, anything is possible," said Christopher Reeves.

Walking on the grounds of the Bible school was so pretty; sometimes, I saw deer in the field. It was a real treat some days as there was a white one, which we occasionally saw. At eight am every morning, we had our devotionals led by many different people. We gathered in the worship hall and would have a time of prayer and worship, and scripture would be read. My heart was like a sponge soaking up life during these times. One morning, a scripture was read from the book of Isaiah Chapter 6 v 8: "Then I heard the voice of the Lord saying 'Whom shall I send? And who will go for us?' And I said, here am I, Lord sends me". I asked the Lord where do you want me to go? I remembered what had happened to me on the stairs of the nurses' home. My going took me to Zambia, Uganda, Tanzania, Lesotho, and South Africa. This is when my Yes became a Go. There were so many miles covered, and people met. I did not know I would study for an honour's degree, a master's degree, and a PhD. I did not know a charity would be formed and celebrate over 20 years of work. I did not think I would meet such remarkable people and sing songs in another language. I did not know I would hear stories of suffering, yet I see such vibrant faith. But I did know, "The Lord will always guide you and satisfy your needs in a sun-scorched land" Isaiah Chapter 58 v 11.

Faith is both supernatural and practical. For instance, Matthew Chapter 25, v 40 says, "I was hungry, and you gave me something to eat. I was thirsty, and you gave me something to drink. I was a stranger, and you welcomed me. I was naked, and you clothed me. I was sick, and you visited me. I was in prison, and you came to me". It is so practical, profoundly human, supernatural and yet costly.

The Haven

When arriving in South Africa for the first time, I did not know what to expect. I knew I would be there for three weeks to work as a volunteer at The Haven. A place where children who were AIDS orphans lived and were cared for and a place where people with AIDS were also cared for. It was run by the Rev Jean Underwood and her remarkable team. The Haven was, and is still, located in the Northern areas of Port Elizabeth, a place where coloured people (a distinct people group in South Africa with a rich and unique culture) were forcibly removed under the apartheid regime. Those parts of the city were poor. It was dusty and noisy. My bedroom was in an outbuilding at The Haven. I was escorted to my bedroom every night, where I used to make a cup of tea and lock my door. The days were full of life. The nights were quiet. It gets dark early in South Africa; there is no twilight. I would light a candle in my room and often sit and think, I am in Africa. I would read scripture and sleep.

Occasionally, I heard gunfire; there was no internet or mobile phones.

Mornings had a rhythm; I would wash, dress, go to The Haven, and have breakfast with the children. The routine of life at The Haven was very structured, which benefited the children, many of whom had chaotic lives before coming to live there.

The word Haven means a "place of safety or refuge". This Haven in Port Elizabeth was that, and I would add to this, a place of hope for those who did not have hope. The Haven was a series of buildings surrounded by a fence and a lovely garden. A wall and fencing surrounded an outer garden, and an inner garden had a covered patio so people could sit outside and be sheltered from the sun. The daily routine was the same apart from outings to the beach and other places and when we had visitors.

After breakfast, the children would clean their teeth, line up in a very straight line, leave the main building of The Haven, and go to pre-school in one of the outbuildings in this secure garden. After pre-school, the children would return to the central part of The Haven, where their bedrooms were, put their bags away, wash their hands, and line up for lunch. There were only ever clean plates. The children ate everything that was given to them. After lunch, they would go to the bathroom, wash their hands, lie on the top of their beds, cover themselves with their day blankets, and read or sleep for an hour. After this, they would go to the bathroom, and then they could play outside and do crafts. If the weather was cloudy and wet, we would put a big blanket on the lounge floor, and the children would watch a DVD. They were very lively and good at playing, but sometimes, I could see that they needed some downtime, just like children who don't have AIDS and who need to rest. Sometimes, it was hard to believe they had AIDS.

Some children who lived at The Haven were found abandoned by the side of the road, some were left under the tables in Shaben's (illegal pubs in the townships), and some were abandoned in a hospital. The children had AIDS and were discarded, unwanted, and left uncared for. Their days at The Haven were safe, full of tasty food, toys to play with, comfortable beds, clean clothes, prayer, and much fun. These children were always laughing. When I had finished tasks assigned to me, I would go into the garden with the children. We would lay on our backs, look at the clouds, and make up stories using the shape of the clouds as they changed. At bedtime, reading stories to the children was a delight for them all, a story and a bible story, and then tucking them all up and saying goodnight. There were nine of them. Some struggled to pronounce my name, so I would hear Shallon (rather than Sharron) when entering The Haven every morning. Being hugged by these warm-hearted, kind children daily was heartening and sometimes loud, as they were often excitedly noisy.

One afternoon, the children found me in my room, yep, all nine of them. They were not supposed to do this but seeing them so persuasive in their request of me was lovely. They said, "Come" and took me by the hand. They led me into The Haven to the doorway of a room in which a lady lay dying of AIDS. They said, "Shallon, you must go in and pray." The children never went into the adults' rooms at The Haven. They all stood in the doorway as I walked to the bedside of the distressed lady. When I held her hand, the children began to sing, and as I prayed for her, she became peaceful, and the children were relieved.

The people staying at The Haven all had AIDS. There were no antiretrovirals available at that time (medication for treating AIDS), and people were extremely sick.

The food at The Haven was lovely. It was high in protein and vitamin A and low in fat and sugar. This was conducive to improving the nutritional state of people with AIDS. The children bathed daily, and a lovely moisture cream was applied to their bodies. The Haven was clean and bright, and something was always going on. People brought donations, courses were being run to help relatives and community members caring for people with AIDS, counselling sessions happened, crafts were made, gardening occurred, and my favourite time was our church service on a Friday. The children's favourite song was "Be bright in the corner where you are, be bright in the corner where you are, where you are, where you are, where you are, where you are, where you are" ... They sang this over and over, using tambourines, guitars, and whatever instruments they could find. It was a joyful sound. The minister would lead a service, and this was always such an encouraging time when we were together.

The Haven was a peaceful place, and I began to feel as the three weeks ended that I should return for longer. What would my family think? I was about to be promoted in my job as a senior staff nurse at the Royal Alexander Sick Children's Hospital in Brighton.

My evenings after the children went to bed were quiet and without distraction. I began to think, if this place were not here, what would happen to these children? They were not AIDS orphans anymore to me. They were children. Funny, cheeky, charming, playful, and full of life. I began to think about returning; how could that happen? Sometimes, scripture speaks into your thoughts; this was one of these times. James Chapter 1 v 27 says, "Pure religion before God the Father is to look after widows and orphans and to keep oneself from being polluted by the things of the world". As I read this, I knew I was to come back and continue to play my part in looking after these children. I had been changed and my yes became another go.

Within a week of returning home to the UK from this initial three-week trip, I had rented out my home, arranged six months of unpaid leave from my job, and communicated to my family that I was returning to South Africa for six months to continue working at The Haven.

My second trip to The Haven lasted for six months, and it had a similar rhythm to the previous trip apart from visiting a lady in Kwazakhele township, going to Lesotho, and using Tea Tree Oil.

The Rev Jean Underwood developed a wellness program for people living with AIDS. It centred around forgiveness, a good diet, good hygiene, vitamin supplements, treating infections with antibiotics, and rest. Jean received a call from a home care team asking for help. We packed the car with clothes, food, medicines, and porridge and drove into Kwazakhele township.

This was my first trip to the township. We arrived at a home near Njoli Square. It was busy, dusty, and noisy as we drove to the home we were about to visit. I will call her Mama Iris; I remember her lovely smile and the sun streaming through her front door. Jean sat with Mama Iris. I sat on a chair in the living room. There were lots of children. Mama Iris was a widow and had lost three of her children to HIV/AIDS. Each time one of her children died, she would take her grandchildren into her home. She now had nine grandchildren to take care of, as well as caring for her terminally-ill daughter with AIDS, who also had children. Mama Iris wept. Jean spoke quietly to her, and we unloaded the car. One of the children climbed onto my lap, and we all prayed. Jean made calls to request help from the home care team to visit Mama Iris's daughter. They arrived and were able to provide immediate care and food.

I know for sure that day I gained an insight into the scripture: "Pure religion before the father is this to visit widows and orphans" James Chapter 1 v 27. This trip to Mama Iris became an experience I will never forget. As I write this, I vividly remember that day. I do not think we spoke on the way home to Jean's house that night. What stayed with me is that we had visited one family, but for Mamas living in these communities, this was the everyday reality of what AIDS was doing to their families. Mama Iris, like so many other Mamas, was simply remarkable. Her heart was broken and overwhelmed, but she, too, knew her heart's strength lay in her heavenly father's hands. "He is father to fatherless and defender of the widow" (Psalm 68 v 5-6). I prayed earnestly for this family, and Jean continued to help them.

Jean and I also visited Lesotho. We took a jet to Jo'burg and a propellor plane to Lesotho. We stayed with a missionary couple who had so many books. Jean was leading the wellness course, and I helped to facilitate the workshop groups. Judy (the lady in whose home we were staying) had communion at a local church with a straw roof every morning and evening. It was a big church built in a wide-open space. It was made of wattle and daub and furnished with wooden benches and chairs. There was an altar with a single candle, which she lit during every service. The days were full of meeting new people, praying, and listening.

I heard things I never expected to hear and listened to the anguish of many young people who were diagnosed with AIDS. They struggled with fear, shame and rejection. They were desperate to be reconciled to God and to help others. It was a profoundly moving time. Jean led communion on the completion day of this program and encouraged people to sit and pray at the altar in the middle of this church. Jean spoke about God being light. I sat quietly in the church, and as people knelt at this altar, they wept. We waited together in the church, and these beautiful people testified that they no longer had sadness but hope. Those who needed to forgive another person who had betrayed them found they could and said they felt light and had peace. It was a time when heaven touched the earth, and endless hope entered people's hearts. The scripture I prayed in the morning of this day was James Ch 4 v 8: "Draw near to God, and he will draw near to you". I saw the God of endless hope do this in the lives of people we met in Lesotho. On my last night in Lesotho, I slept in a rondavel house with a gap between the walls and the roof. It was minus three degrees outside, and there was no heating. I had a Lesotho blanket and have never been so grateful for a blanket. It was so cold, but the morning light as I went outside was magnificent. We were high in the Lesotho mountains, so the sky was a beautiful blue, and we could feel the warmth of the morning sun, even though the ground was frozen and covered with snow.

The following morning, after this course had finished, we were taken to a hospital. It was a maternity hospital. I went to the neonatal unit and found premature babies nursed in incubators made of wood covered with a Perspex lid. The incubator had a thin wooden floor under which was a light bulb. This is how the premature babies were kept warm. These incubators differed hugely from the highly technical ones I nursed premature babies in when I worked in neonatal Intensive care in the UK. I took the "Where There Is No Doctor" book and a copy of the child-to-child education program. I gave these to a doctor at this hospital and explained the program to him. He felt they would be helpful for his work in the community.

We returned to South Africa, where I had a couple of rest days before returning to The Haven. One morning during my devotionals, I read Revelation Chapter 22 v 22, which reads, "The leaves of the trees are for the healing of the nations". Just hold this thought, and all will become clear. It was good to see the children again, who were only too keen to tell me all that had been happening. We spent time together catching up, and I had been informed that the children had been to a farm to visit animals, which had excited them no end. It was lovely to see such joy and gratitude.

I have always been a fan of Tea Tree Oil and still am. I have used it on flea bites, spider bites, spots, abrasions, infected ear lobes, and infected tummy buttons of colleagues when I worked in neonatal intensive care. When I bathed the children at The Haven, they spoke about the pimples on their skin. So, I started to read about Tea Tree Oil (TTO); considering I was using a dial-up internet connection, it took time to complete a lot of reading. I read what I could, then drove to a health shop on Cape Road to consult with a homeopathist to find out what they knew about using it on the skin of people with AIDS.

Writing a proposal was a new venture. I wanted to translate the new-found knowledge into a straightforward approach for a skincare regime for the children. I mixed TTO into aqueous cream and made a two per cent TTO cream, which I used on my shin for a week to try. I found information about how it treats herpes, skin infections, and ringworms. I put a proposal together and sought approval from the board of The Haven to trial using a Tea Tree Oil skincare regime for the children. The nurses at The Haven also began to use it on their hands and loved it.

This involved using Tea Tree Oil soap, putting three drops of a 100% solution of Tea Tree Oil into the bath, the children using a two per cent aqueous and Tea Tree Oil mixture as a skin moisturiser, not for their faces, of course, and then a ten per cent Tea Tree Oil solution mixed in olive oil for skin infections, namely ringworm, scabies, and herpes.

Explaining this to the children required help from a local nurse at The Haven. The nurses informed the children they had also been using it, which led to many questions being asked. Then, I drew body maps for the children who sat drawing pictures of their pimples on their body maps and measuring them with a paper tape measure. We measured the ringworm and herpes lesions on the children's skin. Every Monday, we drew new skin maps using these measurements. They loved their Tea Tree Oil as it smelt fresh. We were all astonished at the results. Week after week, children's pimples were reducing, ringworm patches disappeared, herpes skin infections improved, and the children loved it. This regime continued after I left. Indeed, "the leaves of this tree were healing for these children's skin".

I was asked to type up this project, which I did, and I completed it with the body maps included and anonymised. I took this to the university and met with Dr Jill von der Marwitz, a primary health care lecturer at the NMU who was interested in AIDS care. The university was situated at the city's far end with a fantastic view of the bay. She looked through my notes, and we began to talk. She asked about my trip to Uganda, and I showed her a copy of the child-to-child education program (5) I had used in Uganda. She told me about the children living in the Kwazakhele township who live in child-headed households. As I recall, this was my first time hearing about child-headed households. I was nearing the end of my six-month stay in South Africa and was unsure about the next steps other than going home and picking up my job as a senior staff nurse at the Royal Alexander Children's Hospital. However, Dr von der Marwitz asked if I would consider returning as a student studying in their Advanced Primary Health Care Hons program and as the research part implementing and evaluating the use of child-to-child education with children living in child-headed households in Kwazakhele. It was a beautiful evening as I drove back Jean's home from the university. I remember thinking, "Let not be my will but your will". Could it be that I was about to resign from my job?

Thirteen months later, I left my home and family in the UK and moved to become a student at NMU, where I began working with widows and orphans in the township communities. I had peace, but this yes felt different. It was as if I knew my life would change, and the only way for me to go was forward.

A fact about Tea Tree Oil

Tea Tree Oil, also known as melaleuca oil, is an essential oil obtained by steaming the leaves of the Australian Tea Tree.

Chapter 3
Tuesdays Became Wednesdays and Thursdays...

"Yellow is not an in-between colour; you are either all in yellow or not."

– Author unknown

The wonderful thing about writing a book is that you can skip things. I found settling back in the UK hard after my six-month trip to The Haven and learned quickly to be patient and not say too much when so-called "first world" problems arose. This caused me to feel hidden at times. I prayed for the children and Jean every day. It was beautiful to know this excellent work was happening in tandem with my life in leafy green Sussex. Life during this time was consumed with work, preparing to rent my home out, packing up my life, and reassuring those around me that this was the right path for my life this season.

Of course, I had my doubts and fears I was addressing in this process. During this time, I read many biographies of Amy Carmichael, Festo Kivengere, Mother Teresa, and George Muller. These amazing people's lives helped me stay focused, and I was hugely encouraged by their faith journey. I was inspired by them and grateful for their openness in sharing their challenges and miracles. I think experiencing challenges and miracles go hand in hand. Without challenges and impossibility, there would be no need for miracles.

The day came, however, to leave for South Africa; I put the last things in the loft, packed my suitcase, locked the door and went to the airport to fly to South Africa to become an enrolled student in the Honours program in Advanced Primary Health Care at NMU and to begin visiting women who had become widows and children who were AIDS orphans living in Kwazakhele township.

I took off in winter from London and landed in summer in Port Elizabeth. The evenings were beautiful, and the days were hot.

I was grateful for some time to recover from a hectic time packing and saying goodbye to everyone. In South Africa, we were still using a dial-up internet connection, and mobile phones didn't have WhatsApp or 3G, just expensive text messaging, So I had to limit myself regarding how many I could send. However, I emailed and made regular calls home. I have always loved reading scripture and could sit in the garden, read, walk on the beach or meet with friends I had previously made in South Africa. I loved walking to the beach at Sardina Bay. It was beautiful.

I mostly felt grateful but, at times, apprehensive, too. I settled into church quickly and was part of a great "Life Group". This group is a smaller group of church members who meet regularly. I was in Aunty Cathy's "Life Group", an amazing 80-year-old woman full of faith. She came into the townships with me and encouraged me so very much. She and her husband had seen many miracles in their life and ministry, and she was my friend. I used to pick her up from her home, and we went for coffee together. She loved strong black coffee; she was fun to be with. She always told me, "You must fight the good fight of faith, Sharron".

Then the day came: I registered at NMU as an undergraduate student. On this day, I met other international students, which was encouraging. I went to a classroom to pick up my first allocated textbooks and drove home. It was now very real; I had a timetable, too. My university classes were all day on Monday and other days, too, and on a Saturday morning once a month for four hours.

At the start of the academic year, I began reading the book of Ephesians. One morning, I read Ephesians Chapter 2 v10: "For we are God's handiwork created in Christ Jesus to do good works which God prepared in advance for us to do". I started to pray about what these good works I was to do. We have all heard these quotes about how you eat an elephant or begin a journey with just one bite and just one step, but it feels different when it is your first step and your first bite. I had to learn to walk in my faith shoes for this journey into good works. I was not alone but felt lacking. One evening, when I was grappling with such thoughts, a still, quiet voice spoke the words to my heart: "You did not choose me, but I chose you" John Chapter 15 v 16, the next part of this verse is that you will bear fruit... fruit that will last. Suddenly, my heart was still, and I chose to believe, not to doubt but to believe.

I quickly settled into the routine of church, studies, friendship, and reading, lots and lots of reading. I had weekly tests at university, and studying in the heat was challenging; I also had a new struggle of being homesick. When it hit, it was dreadful. Everyone felt so far away because everything felt so different this time. The question from everyone was, how long will you be in South Africa? Initially, I said I did not know, then I would say my course finishes in two years. Two years felt like a long time. I had never been away from home for so long. In the first few months, I learned to cope with homesickness. The days were ok, but the evenings and nights were challenging. I had many dreams of home. It used to hit me that everything was foreign, and I felt foreign. I was not South African but British. I was a stranger and a bit of a novelty.

It got better in time but was difficult for the first year. You know the saying if you are afraid, do it anyway. I told myself you are homesick, but do it anyway, so I did. By God's grace, the intense feelings of being homesick subsided, and I found comfort and strength in my new routine. I used to go for a run in the evenings, and that helped, too. I spent the evenings studying. I had a visit from my Mum, and suddenly, many people from home wanted to visit. I loved this. My two worlds began to come together. I had not anticipated this, but I was deeply grateful for God's mercy and the generosity and kindness of my family and friends who came to visit. It helped me so much.

I stayed with Dr Jill von de Marwitz and her family in Summerstrand, as Jean had moved to Somerset East, which is not in Port Elizabeth. Being with Jill and her family was much easier as it was close to the university. I used to cycle to university, which I loved, as unlike in England, I never had to wear a coat.

I had been in South Africa for about two months when the day I was to meet Mr. Nikelo came. Mr. Nikelo was a

Kwazakhele Health and Welfare Forum member and the link person between this forum and NMU. I asked for advice before meeting him and was only told to wear a dress or a skirt, no jeans. I woke that morning with the scripture, "Be anxious for nothing, but in all things, with prayer and thanksgiving, make your requests known to God" Philippians Chapter 6 v 7.

During this meeting, My Nikelo and the community invited me to start a Bible study group for widows living in the township. These women had lost their children to HIV/AIDS and were now responsible for caring for their grandchildren. These ladies were the GoGos.

On the following Tuesday morning, I drove to Kwazakhele, keeping the sea on my right-hand side, turning left onto the freeway, then taking a left off the freeway, turning right into Kwazakhele, and meeting Mr Nikelo outside Centenary Hall. This time was pre-sat nav and Google Maps, so I had to remember how to drive into and around Kwazakhele. Thankfully, I was blessed with a good sense of direction. I met Mr. Nikelo, and we went to the second turning left and continued straight along this road to the sports hall, then we turned slightly left. He told me I was meeting a group of GoGos in a board room, and what he did not tell me was it was a board room in a detention centre for young offenders. We were, however, separate from the young offenders in this building and I was grateful for the space we were given.

We parked and went into this room, and the rest, they say, is history. I was greeted with singing, clapping, and joy. Over the years, I've learnt to sing in Xhosa and to speak a little. On this day, though, I listened. These GoGos sounded beautiful, and Mr. Nikelo interpreted

Xhosa into English for me. The ladies spoke freely, cried, laughed, and shared. It was an honour to hear them. They shared their deepest struggles with a stranger, repeatedly saying, "God has sent you to us". I felt humbled to be in the presence of faithful, honourable women.

During this first meeting, I shared Psalm 91: "He who dwells in the shelter of the Highest will rest in the shadow of the Almighty". The ladies said that they wanted to meet every Tuesday. They shared with me their need for bread at home. So, I said I would bring bread, milk, tea, and sugar to the next meeting and asked if they could bring a mug from their home. So, Tuesdays became our meeting day. We met for seven years every Tuesday, and I brought many visitors to this group.

While driving home that day, I stopped at the Summerstrand beach. Across Algo Bay, I could see Kwazakhele in the distance. I often stopped and walked on this beach on Tuesdays after these meetings. I used this time to pray for the Mamas and their families and ask God to help me prepare for the following Tuesday. I loved these times, a time to be still, grateful, and reflect. It was difficult to hear and see the hardship these women were experiencing. Hearing the cry of the poor is hard, but it has moved heaven, and it has moved me.

Something happened before the meeting on the following Tuesday. It is easy to write this now, but at the time, it was challenging to do. One night after my first Tuesday in Kwazakhele, I thought, "How can I fund the Tuesday meetings?". I was not allowed to work in South Africa as per the condition of my Visa. Sometimes, I feel judged when I doubt myself. However, I had concerns and doubts about doing more harm than good and about adding to the disappointment people had already experienced. I was receiving some money from my church in the UK. I sat with a cup of tea at the kitchen table, not unlike sitting at the kitchen table in my flat in the UK and wrote my letter to the Rev Jean Underwood asking if I could volunteer at The Haven. My prayer was the Lord help. I was praying one morning and recalled the scripture, "It is more blessed to give than to receive," Acts Chapter 20 v 35. So, the question was, how much should I give? I felt to give 40 per cent of the money I was receiving to begin the work with the Mamas. So, I went to the cashpoint at Standard Bank in Summerstrand Village and drew out 40 per cent of my money. I got a receipt book and an envelope, put the money in this envelope, and marked it Tuesdays. I then went and sat in "Friend's Coffee Bar" in the Summerstrand village, had a cup of coffee, and looked out to sea. This part is easy to write now as we have known continual provision for over 20 years. Some might say well, of course, but carrying responsibility can be more of a challenge. There has never been a month in these 20-plus years where we have not given to our beneficiaries. As a child, I often prayed, "Our Father in heaven". Who is this Father in heaven? I know him to be "father of the fatherless and defender to the widow". It's who He is.

On the following Tuesday, I woke up early. I had been taught much at bible school in the classes I had attended and read much about God's faithfulness. I started to prepare a bible study on Ephesians Chapter 1. "You are God's workmanship created for good works, chosen in him before the world's creation." I took twenty-five per cent of the money in the envelope marked "Tuesday" and made my way to the shop. I bought loaves of fresh bread, some pieces of cooked chicken, and cartons of milk, tea, coffee, and sugar, which I put into big containers. I also bought some spoons and napkins. I purchased some Xhosa Bibles, too, just in case. All this fitted into the boot of my car, and I began the drive to Mama Nothemba's house. This was my first drive into the township on my own. I found Mama Nothemba's home with ease and parked outside. She had a beautiful home with a polished stoop (doorstep) and pink flowering plants planted in a neat border beside this polished pathway leading to her front door. The grass was green. I walked to the front door and was let in by her son. Mama was sitting on the sofa. I was invited to sit down and have a cup of tea, which I did. It was hot as it was the end of summer. I met her daughter and son at the front door of her home. Mama began to sing and pray. She looked lovely, and I helped her into my car.

My first visit

We drove to Mama Nothemba's sister's home, which was also in Kwazakhele but too far for Mama to walk. I helped Mama out of the car and walked her to her sister's front door. We were invited in. There was much joy and singing, and the greeting was expressed with much gratitude that both ladies had kept well so this visit could occur. Tomorrow is assumed in my culture but not in the township communities in South Africa. I remember thinking, "What humility;" nothing was taken for granted. We were given more tea, and Mama made Vetkoek (Fat Cakes). These are delicious. They are like doughnuts without sugar, coating, or a jam filling. They are fresh and crunchy with a soft yellow inside. Mama Nothemba made them as a gift for her sister.

Seeing the joy this visit brought to each of the ladies was lovely. I was grateful to be received with generous hospitality and taken on a walk in the small but plentiful vegetable garden in the back garden of this home. I was asked to share a scripture. I shared Psalm 91 in Xhosa Indemiso 91. We all held hands and prayed. Mama Nothemba told her sister about the starting group and invited her sister to come.

I walked Mama Nothemba back to the car and put on the AC. I was so grateful that my car had power steering and AC. We drove to the Enkultesweni Centre and met Mr Nikelo and the ladies; this was our first proper meeting. Mr Nikelo, who had borrowed a hot water urn and cups and saucers, and I put everything in my car on a table in this room. I served the ladies Rooibos and English tea, and much chatter ensued. It was such a delight to see these ladies together and chatting. I sat quietly, watching this delightful chatter unfold, not understanding what was being said. Then suddenly, there was quiet, and Mr. Nikelo said, "Over to you, Sharron". I started the meeting by praying for us all, and the ladies began singing again. It was beautiful and gentle worship. I did not understand the words, but I could feel them. We read from the book of Ephesians Chapter 1. Some ladies began to cry as I spoke about what it was to be chosen. Mr Nikelo interpreted, and some ladies shared more deeply about their struggles and things that had happened to them and their families during apartheid. I just listened. We sat quietly for a few minutes after this, and I was grateful that one Mama began to speak about how she and her family had been saved. She told us Police entered her home with guns to arrest her husband during this dark time in South Africa's history. Mama spoke about praying, and suddenly, the police just left, and they did not return. Listening was important. Another Mama then shared that she had slept well since last Tuesday. A lot of the Mamas said the same. They still tell me this. The two consistent testimonies of the Mamas are that they sleep well after the Tuesday meetings and that family members and people in their communities find jobs out of nowhere.

We prayed, invited God into difficult situations, and simply asked for miracles, peace, comfort, and strength. The ladies took the bread and milk home for their grandchildren, who would eat it when they returned from school. I asked what things I could bring the following week. The ladies requested beetroot spinach, tomato seeds, notebooks, and pens. I then drove Mama Nothemba home. I walked her to the door and started the drive home. I stopped the car, walked along the beach, and returned home. I found the noise of the waves reassuring and calming. I loved to feel the breeze. Walking along the beach helped me let go, be reassured, and become strong again in God's presence. My journal became a life-giving place as I wrote what I had experienced and the testimonies the ladies shared. Tuesday evening became a time to retreat. I usually had a bath and went to bed early to read and wrote in my journal; the faith of the ladies deeply moved me, and I loved listening to them sing.

Chapter 4
Being Seen

"White is too brilliant to be seen, so yellow is its filter and costume, revealing that pure light has both brightness and emotional resonance and depth."
– Richard Grossinger

The Mamas felt seen and knew they were not forgotten; this is what they told me. What a huge encouragement. "Are not two sparrows sold for a penny? And not one of them will fall to the ground apart from the father. But even the hairs on your head are all numbered. Therefore, fear not: you are more valuable than many sparrows," Matthew Chapter 10 v 29-31. I was excited to go into Kwazakhele on Tuesdays. There was so much encouragement for us all. We just became a group; it was not difficult. I travelled to Kwazakhele for two years before having a break and coming home to the UK. During this time, I saw a group of women transformed. Women who were overwhelmed, sad, and full of pain became less sad, stronger, and full of purpose. One day, Mama Mandisa said, "We want to do a group like this in our homes for the community". "Weeping may last for a night, but joy comes in the morning" Psalm 30 v 5. However, I witnessed the weeping begin to cease, and dreams of what could be done to help others in Kwazakhele emerged. To share seven years of meetings would be a challenge for me to write and a challenge for you to read. So, I will share some of the beautiful things that happened in our Tuesday meetings.

Some Wonderful Tuesdays

Mama Mankeya was strong in her Christian faith and full of kindness and generosity. I spoke to the ladies one week about tithing and giving. As a point of note, none of the Mamas ever tithed to the GoGo Trust, nor were they ever asked or expected to do so. Mama Mankeya was bearing testimony in the group that she had begun to tithe her chilies from the plants growing in her garden. She told us she would count to nine and then give away the tenth one. She said she had never had so many chillies on the chilli plants in her garden.

The word of faith spoken to the ladies was particularly wonderful when Aunty Cathy visited. She and the Mamas enjoyed being together. I remember Aunty Cathy speaking to the ladies about "fighting the good fight of faith" (1 Timothy 6 v 12). It sparked something in my heart, and after this rich teaching time, I spent weeks with the ladies, listening to them and exploring their questions about this walk of faith. How could I help them when they were teaching me? I brought visitors from the UK and the local community to this group, and this was always an enriching time. Many times, visitors would sit quietly in the car as I drove them back to my home. Visitors would always comment on how remarkable the Mamas were, how beautiful their singing and how wonderful it was to listen to their heartfelt prayers. Mama Margaret always spoke so well and was full of passion.

We have always given food parcels to the Mamas for Christmas Day. One year, we put everything we had bought in big plastic containers with clip-on lids. Each lady received one of these, which was full of food and other things. The Mamas could keep their bread flour in these containers once they had used all the gifts. This is what they had asked for. Mama Margaret opened her container, and she began to weep with gratitude. It had in it, amongst other things, a pot of jam and English tea and a bar of soap and body moisture cream. The ladies were so grateful. It truly is "more blessed to give than to receive" (Acts 20 v 35). People in the UK wanted to give financially, so in April 2003, we set up the GoGo Trust with the help of a South African lawyer. As I prayed about this, I felt the GoGo Trust would be a funnel through which provision would be poured. That is what it has been. This funnel pours in money every month to beneficiaries who are widows and orphans in Kwazakhele and surrounding township communities in South Africa. Who knew that 20 years later, I would still be able to bear testimony to this beautiful provision? I am so grateful for the kindness and generosity of people,

Mama Esther reminds us that God is good and that Jesus is kind. She had a beautiful friend, Mama Ethel, who passed away, and Mama Esther was sad. She found comfort in Jesus and comfort in the love of our group. She was my friend. Now, the GoGo Trust supports her granddaughter through Julian's Children. Mama Esther was a beautiful, faithful lady. She served her family, her community, and her church. I used to have tea in her home and take her to Mama Mandisa's to meet with a group of ladies who regularly met there. She always gave testimony as to how God had kept her well. She used to sing beautifully and always had a smile. I took many visitors to her home over the years, and they all saw the same things in her as I did. She loved fried chicken. On occasion, I would pick up fried chicken from Kentucky for her and take it to her home. This was a treat she enjoyed as we ate some fried chicken together. Mama came to my master's and PhD graduation at the university. She was wise and helped me navigate complex cultural nuances beyond my experience and understanding. Mama Esther became strong in her faith and consistently said, "Jesus did this, Jesus did that".

Don't steal...

There was a young man whom I will call Siyabonga. Mama Esther told me about him and asked if we could help him. I visited Siyabonga with Mama Esther, and we tried to help him. He wanted to earn some money, so on Tuesdays, he would come to the Tuesday group and help me unload the car, help prepare the room, and clean the room afterwards, and I would pay him for his contribution. Nothing was ever stolen from me in the township, and I was never threatened or harmed. I knew generosity, kindness, and warmth. I grew in confidence that visiting was an enriching experience.

Siyabonga had been unpacking my car and helping for about three months and was continuing to retake his school classes. During one of our meetings on Tuesday, there was a lack of peace. I gave Siyabonga my car keys to get something out of my car, and he returned them to me. I genuinely did not think anything of it. He stayed behind, as usual, to help me load the car and then cleaned the room. When I got into my car, my radio had been stolen. I was upset as my CD case was attached to this system, and my CDs had also been stolen. I played it down as the Mamas were upset that this had happened to me. Mama Esther said, "We will pray, Sharron, and it's ok."

That night, I went to bed and had a dream. I knew that Siyabonga had taken it, and I saw that in my dream, my radio and CD player were on a shelf in a shack between two bottles of white liquid. When I woke up in the morning, my phone rang. It was Mama Esther. She said exactly what I saw in my dream. We agreed to go to his home and ask Tata (an elder in Siyabonga's street) to help us. Tata came to Siyabonga's home with us and woke him up. I asked him if he had stolen my radio and CD player and he said he had not. I then told him about my dream. He said he was sorry and that he would help me. We drove with Mama Esther and Tata to a house near an informal settlement. Siyabonga got out of the car and went into the house. A man came out of the house and asked me about my dream, so I told him. He asked if I would go to the police, and I said I would not if my things were returned to me. Tata and Mama exited the car, and I was left with Siyabonga and this new man.

Mama Esther told me, "It's ok, Sharron, you can go with them. We will wait here. You are safe." So off we drove into the informal settlement. The man in the car was cross with Siyabonga, and he apologised to me. We stopped outside a shack. Siyabonga and the man exited the vehicle. I was then asked to go into the shack. On the top shelf were two bottles of white liquid, my radio, CD player, and CDs. They were given back to me, and I was apologised to by all these men.

We all got back into the car. I dropped the man back at his house, picked up Mama Esther and Tata, and drove Siyabonga home.

Mama Esther and I went to Kentucky together; neither of us could quite believe what had happened, but we had a story to tell. Mama helped me that day; we both knew we had a heaven-sent dream and were thankful. Mama Esther was strong and persuaded. This is but one memory I have of her, and I think she would smile knowing I have written this here. Mama Esther passed away a few years ago, a beautiful woman of love and full of faith. A prayerful and dignified lady. Who lived her life well.

Building a school

Our Tuesday groups became our hub, an engine that began to turn. The life we found as we prayed, worshipped, and read scriptures was life-changing for us all. Together, we found new hope, life, healing, and purpose. I know that a new momentum began very quickly, and I was asked to visit the homes of the Mamas to meet their families and listen to their plans for their communities.

Nobuthembu and Nthombekaya were Mama Evelyn's daughters. Mama Evelyn came to our Tuesday group. She was a friend of Mama Esther's too. At the back of Mama Evelyn's home was an area of land. Nobuthembu and Nthombekaya wanted to run a pre-school. I did not know how this would happen, but we all stood in the backyard on this ground and prayed that our Heavenly Father would provide for us to build a pre-school. As we prayed, I felt a demonstration of our faith would be good, so we began to price the cost of building a pre-school. Tata Simon made his breeze blocks. I had enough money to pay for 30 blocks. In one week, without saying anything to people back home, £6,500 was provided for us to begin to build. At this time, Nobuthembu and Nthombekaya attended a course on becoming pre-school teachers. It was an exciting time. They chose the name Vukukhanye, which means to stand up and shine.

The pre-school was built, pictures were painted on the walls, a food garden was planted, cups and plates were purchased, and paper, pens, paint, and a CD player for music were all placed in this new pre-school. Before the school opened, a team of young people from my church in Port Elizabeth came to help us paint and pray. There was much joy in this school. The curricula were bought, and Nobuthembu and Nthombekaya did an excellent job. We had outings to the beach, and the children grew in their faith as they saw much goodness, ate healthy food and loved to learn. The children loved to show me what they had learnt. The spiritual battle over the pre-school was significant, but the family was strong, and the joy of the children gave us all hope.

One day, I received an urgent call from Nthombekaya, "Sharron, you need to come". So, I went to pre-school. When I arrived, I found all the children had gone home vomiting, and Nthombekaya told me the toys in the pre-school had just started blinking on their own. This made me a little perturbed, so I telephoned a local pastor. I understood during this call that church congregation members had previously experienced this; although it wasn't commonplace, it was known to occur. A couple of pastors were sent to the school. We began to pray and sing. Andrew, one of the pastors, felt we should have communion. Suddenly, we all felt peace. Nthombekaya saw two black shapes, like snails without shells, leaving the building. It was about 2pm. Nthombekaya and Nobuthembu felt reassured.

I called the following morning to make sure all was peaceful. Nthombeyaka told me that the parents of the children who had gone home vomiting said to her that the children had stopped vomiting at about 2pm the day before. We later discovered that a cleaner cleaning the pre-school was a practising witch doctor and had used muthi (a witch doctor's potion) to clean the school. Every morning after this, Nobuthembu and Nthombekaya start the day with prayer. I had much to learn. Peace had returned to the pre-school, and the children were settled; we also got a new cleaner. The scripture I began to read and pray through was Ephesians Chapter 6 v 12. "We do not wrestle against flesh and blood but against the rulers, against the authorities, against the cosmic powers over the present darkness, against the spiritual forces of evil in the heavenly places."

Generosity

I was asked what we needed on a trip home to the UK. I told people a jungle gym for the pre-school children to play outside. This was also a journey of faith. Enough money was provided for us to buy a jungle gym and to put a shade over the jungle gym so the children were protected from the sun. Some friends from church in Port Elizabeth dug up grass from their farm and laid a beautiful grass area for the jungle gym to be assembled on. A sand pit was also built. I loved seeing people come together to serve and to help. The generosity of people has always been such a huge encouragement to me. Over the 20-plus years of the GoGo Trust's work, I have been astonished by people's generosity. One Christmas, a friend from South Africa called me. She and her husband had saved money to buy a pool table for their children as a Christmas present. She told me that her children didn't want to receive gifts over Christmas but wanted to give the money to the GoGo Trust. With this money, we bought a trampoline for the pre-school and used the rest of the money to purchase food parcels to give to our families with this money. What kind and thoughtful generosity.

Growing

Mama Mandisa started coming to our Tuesday group, invited by Mama Esther. Mama Mandisa brought her friends with her, and soon, our meeting room became too small. The centre manager allowed us to use the hall. It was more spacious. Mama Mandisa invited me to her home and, after some persuasion, I went. I hesitated, not because I didn't want to, but because my time was becoming thinly stretched. My studies were becoming more demanding, and the work of the GoGo Trust was growing.

Mama Mandisa had a lovely big in-home in Zwide township and asked me to start a group in her home, Zwide township neighbours Kwazakhele township. I had peace about starting this group, so we began on Wednesday afternoons. The ladies attending this group were very strong in their faith, and I wondered what I could bring them. I always felt humbled going to Mama Mandisa's home when I met with her and the ladies attending this group. James Chapter 2 v 5-8 reads, "Has God not chosen those who are poor in the eyes of the world to be rich in faith?" I was learning more than I was teaching. Every week we met, the Mamas would start by saying, "Thank you, Lord, that you kept us well so that we can meet together," and then "What is the Lord saying today, Sharron?". We read the Psalms, the Epistles, and the Gospels together. One day, we prayed and asked God to give us a vision for the community. The GoGos in this group were also concerned for the children and grandchildren, and the need for employment in the community was significant. Many times, as I was leaving Mama Mandisa's to get into my car, I would be approached by people outside and asked to pray. We need to pray that the Lord would help people find jobs continually, and He did. Many came to testify to this.

I want to share a story with you. On the way to her home one Wednesday, I had this scripture in my mind: "God inhabits the praises of his people" Psalm 22 v 3. As I arrived at Mama's house, I was asked if I would mind driving Mama and her friends to another home in another township not too far away. I was informed that one of Mama's friend's daughters was sick with AIDS and had requested we go and pray. Mama Esther was also with us on this day.

We arrived at a lovely home and were met by Mama Mandisa's friend. It was a warm welcome. We were shown into the lounge. I remember this day being hot. We were then shown into a room where Mama's daughter was lying in her bed, so unwell with AIDS. Her breathing was shallow, and she was skeletal. The young lady was too weak to speak, but I remember her lovely smile.

She reached for my hand, which I gently took hold of. The ladies were also invited in, and we surrounded her bed. I had been in South Africa for over two years and learned to sing some worship songs in Xhosa. We gently began to praise and worship around this young lady's bed. There was a beautiful sense of peace. I was reminded of the scripture I had in my mind earlier that day and felt we should worship and praise the Lord together. After about half an hour, we left. We were quiet in the car going home to Mama Mandisa's home, and I felt like we had touched heaven.

About six weeks later, I was buying some bread in the Spar at Daku with Mama Esther. A young lady came up to me and asked if I remembered her. I said that I did not recognise her. She then told me what happened to her after we worshipped in her room. This young lady was so sick and skeletal, now walking around in Daku Spar buying bread. I marvelled at how well she looked and how much weight she had put on. She told me it was a miracle, and I would have to agree. This day was so encouraging to us all, and Mama Esther and Mama Mandisa also testified to this miracle in our Tuesday group. We were all astounded and encouraged.

Soup Cells

Shortly after this, our soup cells began, and they continue. The Mamas had asked me to visit each of their homes for a while. They wanted me to understand how their families and community continually looked to them for encouragement, support, and provision. I listened to them during these home visits and began understanding the pressures and challenges they faced daily in these communities. Visiting was time-consuming and challenging and hot but constantly enriching. I used to get up early on Tuesday mornings to pray and prepare for the Tuesday meeting. One morning, I read in the book of Acts Ch 2 v 42-47: "They devoted themselves to the teaching and fellowship and the breaking of bread and prayer". The Mamas wanted to feed community members; they wanted to help. So, I found a product sold through a local supplier of a rich fortified soup with rice. We tried it, and the ladies loved it, so we ordered it, and the soup cells began. They have been running now for 19 years. A lot of soup has been made over the years. The Mamas are given 25kg bags of soup powder fortified with rice and vitamins each month. We also provide the Mamas with money for electricity or gas to cook this soup. I've eaten this soup many times. When I lived in South Africa, I had it for lunch most days as I visited the soup cells often.

The Mamas decided the days they wanted to host their soup cells. They chose to meet in a designated home and devote themselves to fellowship with one another, and they would "devote themselves to the apostles teaching to the breaking of bread and prayer" (Acts Chapter 2 v 42). They would then eat a nutritious soup together and feed community members who needed food. Some Mamas would let families know there would be a warm meal, so when people had been to the clinic for their TB medication, they would come to a soup cell to be able to take this medication with food. Some would feed children who were orphans in their communities living in granny-headed households, so these children had a warm and nutritious meal on their way home from school. Some children would bring a tin and take their soup home.

Some Mamas would transform this soup into a meal comprising spinach and potatoes. Meeting a need in their community eased the burden for the Mamas. They felt less helpless and less overwhelmed. The soup cells became, and still are, an oasis of hope in the communities. Scriptures are read, which have brought hope and life to many, prayers have been prayed and answered, and a delicious soup has been eaten by many.

What I loved was being able to experience first-hand the loving kindness and faithfulness with which these faith-filled Mamas served their community. They were loving God and loving their neighbour. Wednesday was the day of my research methods module at Nelson Mandela University. These lectures were from 5.30pm until 8pm every week on a Wednesday. I used to finish at this soup cell and nap on a bed in Mama Mandisa's home before driving to the other end of the city to the university to attend this class.

Washing feet

Tuesdays were special days; being together with the Mamas, eating, praying, and being encouraged was a privilege. Preparing for these meetings was always an encouraging time. When Annie, a friend of mine, visited from the UK, I asked if she wanted to take the Tuesday meeting. She said yes and felt we should wash the feet of the ladies. This morning, we were joined by an Afrikaans' lady whom I will call Magda. We took bowls, towels, soap, and foot cream. I had felt previously to do this but was concerned it would open deep wounds in the ladies due to what they had experienced during the apartheid era and through experiencing loss. I told Annie my concerns. Annie is a very gentle person and very sincere. I knew it was time to trust. We headed into the township, and Annie met the ladies in our meeting room. Annie shared her scripture about when Jesus washed his disciples' feet.

Magda encouraged the ladies with her own story of forgiveness, and we began to sing softly in Xhosa; then, we began to wash the feet of the Mamas. Magda and Annie knelt and washed the ladies' feet and dried them. I knelt after them and creamed the ladies' feet. No one spoke, but tears ran down the lady's faces. No one spoke for a long time, and we all experienced gentleness and dignity. Mama Mankeya broke the silence. Through a tear-stained face, she said she never believed that white people would wash her feet. She exclaimed that she knew we were all equal in God's eyes. I found this a humbling meeting, and something changed after this day. There was a realisation of value and worth and a new confidence in being seen and understood. The journey of forgiveness is never straightforward. The depth of healing after this time was somehow more significant. Thank you, Annie.

Annie's husband, Peter, also joined us in the township when they came to South Africa on their honeymoon the following year. Peter has a gift of worship. He brought his guitar and worshipped with the ladies at a Tuesday meeting. He was moved, we were all moved, and the ladies felt further encouraged. Thank you, Peter.

Mums with AIDS

After meeting on Tuesdays for about three years, one of the Mamas invited me to visit her home to meet her daughter, who was dying of AIDS. Mama's home was a beautifully kept shack with pink flowers in the yard. It was so clean, and knitted blankets were on all the chairs in the main room. The bedroom was at the back of the shack. It had an open window with a view of the blue sky. It was quiet. I met her daughter, who was in bed and very weak. I will call her Rose. We began to talk, and Rose told me of her heart's desire for her son. I encouraged her to write a letter to him. Her eyes light up. We talked about what she could write. She wanted to write about her childhood memories of him as a baby and a toddler. She wanted to write words of wisdom about what she wished him to know on birthdays, passing exams, starting university, starting work, becoming engaged, getting married, and becoming a father and a husband.

I was with Rose for a couple of hours. We talked, prayed, and shared scripture. I asked if there was anything she would like. She asked for a bar of chocolate, coffee and milk. She wanted to share this with her mum and son. I never thought to bring chocolate. So, I left money to buy these things and paper, pens, and envelopes for Rose to write and leave letters for her son. She passed away four days later.

After this, I was asked to start a group for Mums with AIDS. I think the request came from the Kwazakhele Welfare Forum. These Mums were daughters of the Mamas who came on Tuesdays and who had AIDS.

These Mums and I met weekly for eight weeks. In my mind, I had sensed the word accompaniment. We met in a private room in the centre where the Tuesday meetings were held. I took papers, pens, envelopes, bread, and milk. The ladies liked the bread and the milk. I could see they were unwell and physically weak. Antiretroviral therapy (medication to treat AIDS) roll-out in South Africa was slow at this time. The stigma surrounding AIDS was ever-present for these ladies and their families. The stories were heartbreaking. Stories full of anguish, pain, loss, and shame. After the first week, I asked if the ladies wanted to continue to meet and was met with a resounding yes. They wanted a safe space to share and to pray.

Inspired by Rose's experience, the ladies wrote letters to their children. They cried and laughed. One of the meetings fell on my birthday, so I took a cake and juice, and we decided to celebrate all our birthdays. It was a day to celebrate life. We continued to pray for miracles, and the ladies experienced renewed strength and hope and embraced the journey of forgiveness.

These ladies shared their experiences and thoughts about Heaven; some even had visions of heaven. Heaven felt close in these ladies' words, and I felt honoured that they let me into the anguish of their souls and their dreams and hopes, too. They were concerned for their children who would be left behind and the burden this would place on their mothers. This was the heart lament of these precious women.

Subsequently, I felt compelled to support these children, as the GoGo Trust did before we began Julian's Children, which is the orphan care aspect of the GoGo Trust.

Knowing a food parcel and school fees would be provided for their children brought comfort to these ladies and alleviated some of the anxiety they were experiencing. Speaking to one another in this group made the ladies feel supported and understood. Many times, they told me that they felt safe. This eased tensions in their homes as they knew they had a safe space to speak, which would not distress their children or mothers. This group ran its course. The ladies wrote letters. They were reading scripture regularly and committed to praying for each other daily. As we approached two months together, the ladies decided to meet in each other's homes. Some occasionally came on a Tuesday, but we stopped meeting together. They were accompanied, and I learnt so much from these ladies and started to think about the orphans I was beginning to meet. Heaven for these ladies was a breath away.

Funerals

Before I went to South Africa, I had attended four funerals. The first funeral I attended was of a neighbour who died playing sport. I think it was squash. On that day, I remember thinking, "What would that be like if it were someone you loved?" Then the unthinkable happened. I attended the funeral of my brother. He was 17 years of age. On his 17th birthday, I bought him a gold signet ring. I worked in a jeweller's shop then and got a discount. I am so glad I did, as he didn't see his 18th birthday. I've been asked if I would write a second book. If I did, it would probably be about the journey of grief when the unthinkable happens. But that story isn't for now.

The third funeral I attended was of the first ward sister I worked for in London. The fourth funeral I attended was for a family of a baby who died. A colleague and I went to this funeral. He was a baby boy who had a condition incompatible with life, but he was loved by his family, by my colleagues and me.

Funerals in the Xhosa culture are a family and community affair. Funerals occurred on Saturdays in the township communities and lasted five or six hours. Before the day of the funeral in the home of the person who had passed away, all the furniture is removed from that home. Grieving family members would wear black in the community, and the extended family members would keep arriving at that home. Food was provided, and many prayers were said. Funeral plans usually cover the expense of funerals. When Mama Ethel passed away, I was invited to the family home and was accompanied by Mama Esther. We entered Mama Ethel's home, which was filled with people. I was instructed what to do, so I took my place on the floor. I could feel the sadness of her loved ones. After sharing scripture and praying, we were offered food on a plate and a refreshing glass of juice. The food I was offered had a lovely salad with beetroot and carrots and a surprise of Fried Chickens' Feet with nails. I remember thinking about how you eat around a nail. I started with the salad and watched the others. It would have been rude to refuse, so I just ate. I can't say it was with a grateful heart, but I dare say it was tasty. Mama Esther had her eyes on me and winked. When we got into the car, she told me she never would have believed she would see a white lady eating chicken feet and say they were tasty. We laughed. It brought some light to a sad day.

Mama Esther and Mama Ethel had been best friends. Mama was going to miss Mama Ethel, another beautiful, faithful, kind, and dignified lady. I was invited to so many funerals and attended many. They were long. The order of the day was a service at the home, a service in the church, a service at the graveside, and a meal at the family home on returning from the graveside. I wondered how exhausting they were for the Mamas who attended many more funerals than I did. There was strength and dignity in the services and much singing. There was no escaping facing one's mortality.

I used to think how valuable life is and had written on my heart during this time not to take life for granted. I wanted to live well, not perfectly and without mistakes, but to live it well. One day, we were at a funeral in Missionvale. The service at the grave side concluded, and there was so little space to stand. Many of us had to stand on another grave to hear the service we were attending. The graves were very close to one another. Another funeral I attended was next to the pauper graves. I remember thinking I'd read about pauper graves, but now I have seen some. They had a wooden cross put at the head of the grave. The earth was piled high, and the wooden cross was stuck in the soil. The person buried below was made in the image of God and was a son or daughter at the very least, and maybe more. Let's say that was a moment.

SHARRON FROOD

Chapter 5
Visiting

"Yellow-coloured objects appear to be gold."
– Aristotle

The Mamas had a fresh sense of purpose and were encouraged. Alongside the work of the GoGo Trust, my academic studies continued. For part of my Honours degree, I was implementing a child-to-child primary health care education program for children living as AIDS orphans in child-headed households in Kwazakhele.

Before starting this aspect of my degree, Mr Nikelo asked me to visit a child-headed household in the informal settlement and bring some clean dressings. When I reflect on visiting, I think of many things, some beautiful and enriching, some sad and overwhelming. So, what was the key to a successful visit? Prayer, a word of encouragement, and gifts could be key aspects. Being present is essential, and the phrase accompaniment comes to mind so people feel less lonely and more seen. When I visited these families, I was advised to take eggs, bread, milk, sugar and cool drinks. These gifts were well received, and who doesn't like a cool drink on a hot day? When we visit people, they feel less alone and more visible. When we visit someone in their home, we see them differently. We say I want to spend my time coming to see you. I want to know how you are, and we learn how to spend quality time. A good visit is uplifting for both the visitor and the visitee. When we spend time with people, we connect and engage, and we see the needs of others more clearly. We learn, and we gain insight by being present and listening. I was about to embark on lots of life-changing visits. A new lived experience was made visible to me. I have often felt that we need to visit more and realise the importance of connecting with people afresh.

I brought dressings and porridge called Pronutro to this visit. I love this porridge, and I thought the children would love it too, which they did. On entering the home, there were five children. The eldest child in the family I will call Faith. Faith cared for her brothers and sisters at the age of 17 years. The youngest child, I will call Luyanda. Luyanda had cut his foot on a piece of broken glass, and Faith had cleaned it with paraffin. Luyanda now had a blister covering two-thirds of his foot. She had washed his socks, and he had a pair of shoes to wear. I de-roofed the blister and covered it with a clean dressing. He then put on his socks and shoes. I returned every other day to dress this wound until Faith was confident to do it for him. His foot healed, they loved the porridge, and I never left without praying for the family. I was affected by the poverty and suffering these children endured daily and used to think about them when it rained. I believe this is the day that Julian's Children (the orphans' care aspect of the GoGo Trust) started, but I didn't know that then.

These first visits to children in child-headed households were centred around education. I was teaching primary health care education using the child-to-child education program. The visits I made subsequently were to listen to children who had become AIDS orphans and who were living in township communities in South Africa. Driving through the townships, the needs of people were apparent. I could cope with the smells but struggled with the flies and fleas.

When implementing the child-to-child education program, I first translated it into Xhosa and ensured it was nicely printed and bound for each family. As it was the research aspect of my Honours degree, I had a quiz for the children to complete before the child-to-child education program and a quiz to complete a week after the program was implemented to ascertain their learning.

One of the children's exercises was to tie a stone on a piece of string to give you a flavour of this program. Then, make marks on this piece of string. The longer the piece of string, the slower the stone swung from side to side. The shorter the string, the more quickly the stone began to swing. This was to denote when children needed to go to the clinic for treatment for a worsening respiratory infection. They loved doing this and would make each other lie on the floor, count their respiratory rate, and synchronise it to swinging a stone on a string. If the breathing was fast and the stone was swinging fast (this was marked by a red line on the piece of string), the older child knew the younger child needed to go to the clinic to see a nurse.

Another activity undertaken was regarding germs. I cut out pictures of germs and put the blue tack on the back. The children had to walk around their homes and set these printed germs in places they thought germs were likely to be. We would then talk through how to prevent these germs from spreading. Another activity centred around making rehydration fluid, and another on how to prevent accidents in the home. The children were given pictures of potential hazards, and they had to demonstrate the hazards depicted in the pictures.

This was fascinating and led to much ingenuity among the children regarding how they could make their homes safer. They loved drawing pictures and answering questions relating to their newly-acquired knowledge. I enjoyed these visits; they were enabling for us all. An interpreter accompanied me, and he said he had learned a great deal, too.

The interpreter and I visited ten child-headed homes each time, and we took porridge, eggs, juice, and biscuits. I was usually at each home for five hours during each visit. It took time to go through the program, have lunch together, and walk around the communities where the children lived. My main challenge was with flies and flea bites. Poverty hurts people; it's unkind. Yet, in all this challenge, I developed such respect for the head child in these child-headed households. Who desired to be seen, encouraged, and supported. The question I had was how to strengthen their already developed unique resilience. I began to think more deeply when I drove home to my lovely, comfy home with food in the fridge, a clean bed, friends, and a beautiful garden. My soul, however, wasn't unaffected by what I saw. I knew heaven was turned towards these children. I asked what I could do to help and how this could be sustained.

Nelson Mandela once said, "There is no keener revelation of a society soul than how it takes care of its children".

The Tuesday group continued to flourish, and Faith, the head child in one of these child-headed household families, joined this group. Mama Esther invited her. Faith loved being with the Mamas and showed such respect to them. This made me think that a family requires every generation. Yet, in South Africa, it was as if a generation was lost. The children are grieving for their parents, and the grandmothers are mourning the loss of their child and are deeply affected by the grief of their grandchildren. When children become AIDS orphans and are living in these communities, complex grief and poverty become pervasive. The challenge to keep going is enormous. To live with purpose and to be pulled towards dreams for the future is complex.

There were weeks in our Tuesday group where the ladies just sat as they were just tired. A scripture says, "After you have done all you can, just stand" Ephesians Chapter 6 v 13-14. It was time to encourage the ladies. I used to take time as part of the Tuesday group to help them practice meditation. I taught them to stand up on the inside whilst sitting down in a chair. They loved this. The ladies used to say that they experienced peace and found strength in being. We spoke a lot about the scripture, "Be anxious for nothing but in all things with prayer and thanksgiving make your requests known to God" Philippians Chapter 4 v 6. We talked about many ways of practising this. One way was to sit down and make our request known to God. The Mamas would give over their anxieties, and I would give over my constant fear of not disappointing, not overreaching, and not causing harm.

The Mamas came to all my graduations, and I valued their presence, time, and support. After my first graduation, the question was the next step. There seemed to be an obvious next step, but I needed some advice. After meeting with my Professor in South Africa, it became apparent what the next step was. I had spoken with my professor about my experiences visiting the children living in child-headed households; my professor encouraged me to use a master's degree to tell the stories of these children. Many societal solutions are developed and implemented using a top-down or policy-driven approach. However, when solutions can be created by those experiencing the phenomena, one would assume these could be more successful. I knew it would be challenging, but I was persuaded that visiting orphans and then, with their permission, telling their stories was the next step. So, after filling in many forms and submitting applications, this was the next step: more visiting and more listening. I was ready to start a master's degree.

After a break in the January, registering for the Master's Program at the NMU was more familiar. I had been in South Africa for four years at this point. Life then involved attending research methods lectures, submitting ethical approval applications to the ethics committee at the university, and reading, a lot of reading. The process began with finding a licensed translator who could translate English into Xhosa – undertaking a literature search to identify what was already known and published about children living as AIDS orphans in township communities in South Africa, in addition to continuing with our Tuesday group, soup cells and pre-school. Life became busy.

Chapter 6
Children Become Orphans; They Are Not Born Orphans

"'One Yellow Daffodil' is both a look to the past and the future and expresses my belief in our children's great spirit and strength."

– David Adler

I have always loved to study, so I was either studying the scriptures, research methodology, or principles of ethics about undertaking a research Master's. The four soup cells ran well, and I visited each one every other week. There was a sense of buoyancy in the Mamas at this time. We had found a rhythm, and the Lord kept providing, so we kept doing.

The day came when ethical approval from NMU had been granted, and I drove to meet a certified interpreter and community worker. She had already identified eight families for me to interview. This felt surreal. I had a digital recorder and an interpreter. I was going to embark on a two-month schedule of interviewing children living as AIDS orphans in Kwazakhele and writing up their stories. I knew it would be a challenge, but I did not realise how astonished I would be by these remarkable children.

Mark Chapter 9 v 34 reads: "Jesus put a child amid them and taking him in his arms he said to them 'whoever receives one such child in my name receives me'." I write this here as a big arch of yellow spoken over the lives of these children by their Heavenly Father. This scripture denotes value and truth and gives steadfast hope concerning their lives' value in the eyes of their Heavenly Father. Yet, their present circumstances would be challenging to live, hard to see, and sometimes overwhelming to hear. The paradox of finding hope in a hopeless place and joy during suffering was to be a reality. I had the privilege of these children opening their homes and lives to me.

Atenkosi

The first home my interpreter and I drove to was yellow. It was in a poor neighbourhood, and to get there, the roads were dusty and filled with children playing in the street without shoes on. We met a young man in his house. I will call him Atenkosi. He was 18 years old. I picked up roast chicken, bread, salad, a cool drink, and biscuits from the shops to give him before this visit. He was a self-assured young man but quietly spoken. We walked into his kitchen, which was sparse. There was a table with two chairs. He got glasses and a plate and said he would talk to us in the garage as he did not want the story he was about to tell me to be told in his home. So, we walked to the garage and sat on whatever we could find. I found that all the children I visited wanted to tell their stories. My interpreter, the community worker I was working with, had known Atenkosi for several months. He had collapsed in school after the death of his mother, as he kept going to school without anything to eat. On day four of going to school without eating, he collapsed, and the community worker visited him. Once he began to speak to me, he couldn't stop. I made some notes, but everything was recorded and transcribed on a digital recording device. When I transcribed this interview, it took up over 20 pages. He did not know his Mum had AIDS, but he knew she was unwell. One day, she went to the hospital, and she did not come home. He loved his Mum very much, and she instilled in him the need to go to school and do his homework, which he did. He was bright, articulate, and determined. I remember him saying, "When I became an orphan, it was like a tree of pain and difficulty grew inside me. I wanted someone to put their hand in my mouth and rip out this tree because I didn't want it."

He found hope in going to school, talking about the future, reading and learning, and loved to watch football. He said he knew he had a Heavenly Father and wanted to live a good life. After he had finished school, the GoGo Trust supported him in going to college. Before taking his place, he worked at a local supermarket and stacked the trolleys in the car park. One day, a man left his wallet in the shopping trolley with all his cards and R2000 (approx. £85) in cash. Atenkosi went to his supervisor and handed it in. The man was notified by the store manager, who then came to the store to collect his wallet. He wanted to meet Atenkosi. This man met Atenkosi and gave him R500 out of his wallet. The man asked him, "Why didn't you take the cash?". Atenkosi told him, "Because I wanted you to have hope that if you lose something in South Africa, it can be returned to you". The man cried and said that Atenkosi had given him hope. Atenkosi is now a businessman in Johannesburg, and recently, when I was in South Africa, he met me at the airport with a beautiful card and gave me a bottle of perfume. I felt so proud of him. He kept moving forward. He became a kind and loving man. He never stopped loving and moving forward.

In his own words

> "All I can say is it's like I have a deep pain inside since I became an AIDS orphan; I have no words to say how it feels. I have no one to go to help me. Sometimes I want to die." (Atenkosi)

> "The thing that affects me the most is the loss of my mother's care. She was always encouraging me and sharing ideas with me. I miss those kind words of encouragement and hope. She was always patient and kind. I miss her meeting me from school." (Atenkosi)

> "When my mother was alive, and my brothers were at home, I liked being at home with them. We used to help with the cooking, and it was a lovely, fun time. We just liked to be together. Now I don't like to be home. It's empty and a sad place to me now. It's like the life has left my home." (Atenkosi)

> "When my mother was sick, I used to wash her and make her to be comfortable. I was sad because she was sick, but it was also a nice time because she was at home, and we did have a nice time together. I felt good to help her. I am sad she has died. I miss her." (Atenkosi)

> "When I do come home from school, there is no food. It was never like that before. When my mother was alive, there was always food in the house. Now, if I don't cook, I don't eat. In February last year, I didn't eat for four days. I come home from school. I drink water, and I lie in bed to sleep. When I am hungry, I drink more water and sleep again. This

angers me because I can't learn at school when hungry." (Atenkosi)

"The one thing I miss is my mother's cooking. It's difficult now to always have food to eat. Sometimes our neighbours they do cook food for us. If they don't have food, we don't eat, and we go to bed hungry. The worst is to eat cold leftovers. It was not like that when my mother was alive." (Atenkosi)

"Sometimes I feel like I did just come from the water." (Akenkosi)

"I was thinking who will now take me to be their son because I don't even have clean clothes to wear." (Atenkosi)

"My home is not my home anymore since my mother died. The life of my home has died, and now I am staying alone and taking care of myself." (Atenkosi)

"Once, I went to my aunt for help. She told me I was not her child, so she could not help me. It makes me sad that I don't belong to anyone. There is no love like your mother's and father's love because you did come from them." (Atenkosi)

"I ask myself what a person can do without money (Atenkosi)

There is often not enough money for food, so how can I buy other things we need?" (Atenkosi)

"I felt humiliated sometimes at school because I had no money. Just this week the teacher said we must each bring R2.00 to contribute to buying cleaning products for cleaning the classroom. I didn't have

R2.00, so the children in the class did shout at me. I feel humiliated because of this. I also feel small because I can't pay school fees. When the teacher keeps asking, I feel so poor because I can't pay. Last month there was a trip to a museum. I didn't go because I had no money to pay for that trip. So, I did stay at my home that day." (Atenkosi)

"Some children laugh at me at school because I never have food to eat. I don't even have a few cents to buy an apple with. So, I sit in the classroom alone at the break. It's better like that. In February I had no food for four days because I decided to go back to school, so I can't work in the day. One of my neighbours did see what I was doing and gave me food in the morning and evening, so I could get an education." (Atenkosi)

"After my mother died, I struggled to get food and clothes. One day, I did steal washing from the washing line in a house far from mine. I stole the top because it was nice and gave me status in the community. I stole most of my clothes like this. One day, I did get caught. I did community service for six months. I had to clean the Empilweni TB hospital. It was too terrible. I don't steal anymore." (Atenkosi)

"Sometimes, I was going to the local shop, and I did steal sweets just because I wanted to. I used to think about breaking into houses to take things other people have that I don't. I decided not to do that. I just steal sweets to eat." (Atenkosi)

"After the death of my mother, I did hang out on the street with my friends. They did give me dagga to smoke. I did like it because it made the burning anger in me go down, and I did feel peaceful." (Atenkosi)

"I don't worry about stealing when I am high. I just steal because then I am brave, and even if I am caught, I won't feel pain. It is like that." (Atenkosi)

"I feel like I have a pain deep in my chest. If I could take hold of it and pull it out it would be much better. But nothing does take that pain away since my mother did die. Even when I cry, it is still there; sometimes, it burns in my chest." (Atenkosi)

"After the death of my mother, I did feel too sore in my heart. The only thing that does make me forget that pain is dagga. When I smoke it, it makes the pain in my heart numb, and then I feel better again." (Atenkosi)

"Everyone just left me. My mother died, my aunt took my brothers, and I was just left to take care of myself without any money. I wanted to die because I did think I was now living in hell." (Atenkosi)

"My home is lonely now; my mother has died. When I come home from school, there is no one there. I am alone. It is like that now. I feel lonely because of this." (Atenkosi)

"The day my mother did pass away was like a bad dream to me. I felt like a deep pain inside, and I cried and cried." (Atenkosi)

"Following the death of my mother, I thought I was going mad. I kept seeing her everywhere, but I knew she was dead." (Atenkosi)

"I never knew a person could cry so much. I didn't understand a person can make so many tears. I cried like a baby after the death of my mother; I just cried and cried." (Akenkosi)

"No one did care for me after my mother died. No one did even call to see how we were. No one did take care of us, no one. We did suffer too much because of this." (Atenkosi)

"The worst day of my life was when my mother did pass away. She was caring nicely for us. When she did die, all the caring we knew died too. It was like that. No one did care for us." (Atenkosi)

"I was never angry before. I was peaceful. Now sometimes I feel like a war inside my stomach; I just want to punch something." (Atenkosi)

"The day my mother did die, I was very angry with God that he did take her. I still needed her, and he took her. Sometimes I shake my fist at him and shout. 'Why, God, why?" (Atenkosi)

"After the funeral of my mother and everyone went, I was just alone. I didn't know what to do, so I just sat on my bed, and I did cry. I was under a waterfall of bad things that kept falling on my head." (Atenkosi)

"One day after my mother did die, I was at the school. I couldn't breathe. It was like something burning in my chest. It was bad. I was sweating and cold. So, I did go outside my class and I did breathe. It was fear. I was terrified because my life was too hard now. But it's better now because I know I can keep going to school." (Atenkosi)

"I was afraid because I was uncertain if I could continue my studies. I didn't know who would buy school uniforms for me or pay my school fees." (Atenkosi)

"When I had to make decisions about my matric subjects, I didn't know what to do. I had no parents to ask and no one to go to. I did feel very insecure." (Atenkosi)

"It's too hard for me since my mother did die. I also just want to get out of this life too." (Atenkosi)

"Many times, I wanted to kill myself after my mother passed away. One day, I did go the garage to kill myself, but I just sat there. I couldn't do it." (Atenkosi)

"Something kept telling me not to give up, so each day I did keep going. Sometimes I wanted to die, but I didn't want to kill myself because then I had no future, and I wanted a future." (Atenkosi)

"I did find it difficult at first to accept help from my friend. After my mother died, I had no clothes to wear. My friend told his mother, and she brought me a pair of trousers. It was hard to accept it from him, but I did have a trouser with no holes, and that made me glad and made me have hope as I don't look poor." (Atenkosi)

"My friend reached out to me and helped me, and that gave me hope because I didn't feel alone anymore. I felt like my worries mattered to my friend, and that made me know I have a future." (Atenkosi)

"I have a hope that I can overcome the death of my mother because when I cry, my friends listen; they try and understand and help me. They encourage me that I can still be a politician one day." (Atenkosi)

"Whenever I went to church, God talked to me. The minister spoke and answered many questions, so I started to pray to God because I needed miracles." (Atenkosi)

"When I am at school, I am like everyone else. I am doing my studies, and I am always talking about the future. This is good for me because I like to learn. Education is power, and when I leave school, I want to be a social worker to help people suffering, like me." (Atenkosi)

"My teacher is telling me I am clever because I do all my homework and pass the tests. This makes me feel good inside. I have hope for the future if I work hard in my studies." (Atenkosi)

Akenkosi completed his Grade 12 education and became a businessman. His most delightful quality is that he has remained loving and open. His encouragement to us is to remain loving.

Faith

Our next visit was to the informal settlement, where we visited Faith's home. She had asked me specifically to interview her. The children in her family were all at school, apart from her baby brother, who was three years old, playing in the yard with his friends. We drank cool drinks together, and she had some bread to eat.

She wanted to pray before she spoke to me, so we prayed. She began to speak freely. Faith was 17 and responsible for caring for her four siblings. She cooked, cleaned, made sure they did their homework and tried to provide for them. An aunty dropped some food at their home when she could, and the neighbours brought leftovers for the children to eat every evening. The home was very poor, with bare mud floors and a small kitchen area. She told me how they lived mostly out of one bowl of food, which they shared in the evening with a single spoon, but they were grateful for the food they did have.

Faith took much pride in the fact that the children who went to school were doing well, and each had a clean school uniform. I wasn't prepared for what she was about to disclose, but I felt grateful she did. She said, "I want to feel clean..." Then she just told us she has sex with men in the community for 60 rand (approx. £2.50) so that she can buy food for the children. She cried... we listened. This was the day we had our first Julian's Children family to support. We had a regular donation to the GoGo Trust now from Stonehouse church. After finishing the interview, we went to the supermarket to buy food and ensured that food was given to this family weekly. Faith didn't have to have sex to provide food for her family anymore. Faith asked for stamps and paper. She wrote a letter to her uncle, who then stepped in to help the family financially, and he began to support them. Faith regularly came to the Tuesday meeting, found much peace and healing and light in the darkness, and shame left her life.

In her own words

> "No one in my family came to see me. I am just now left alone to care for myself, and I don't even know how to make bread." (Faith)

> "I feel so low when the neighbours just give me food and my friends' old clothes. I hate being poor; sometimes, I look terrible. Sometimes, people laugh at me; it wasn't like that when my father was alive. Now it's like that. I am sad that we are alone. No one wants to help us. It is like that. I feel humiliated, and I feel sad." (Faith)

> "I used to do everything for my mother. I would collect her money from the bank and look after her when she was sick; I used to wash her and help her go to the toilet. I used to lift her from the bed to a bucket so she could go to the toilet. Then go and empty it. I used to do all the washing, and I used also to wash my mother. She used to sleep on my bed with me. I like that. I miss her being here with us." (Faith)

> "My father was just coughing all the time. My sister and I did care for him. She washed his top, and I did wash the bottom parts. I take him to the toilet because he is too weak. My sister washed him and fed him. I cleaned the house and yard. I used to buy rubbing stuff for his chest from the chemist. I used to rub it on him, and then he got better. One day, the

breath did go out of him. When that did happen, my hope did go away." (Faith)

"When my father was alive, he always gave us food. Now he is dead; I must go to the neighbours and beg for food. The horrible thing is if the neighbours ask you in their home for a meal. This is too bad. Then I do feel sad because I know that my brothers and sisters at home don't eat." (Faith)

"After the death of our mother, we don't eat every day. Sometimes we don't eat for three days. When my grandmother was alive, it was not like that. She made porridge for us for school and dumplings when we came home from school. She always cooked for us in the evenings. I don't like being hungry. I didn't know this hunger when my grandmother was alive." (Faith)

"None of my family members offered to help me after my mother died. They just left after the funeral, and they could see we were struggling, and no one was taking care of us. They tell us we don't belong to them, but we belong to God." (Faith)

"I am ashamed about what I am to tell you. When my father did die, I was very alone. We were six children and had no money for food. Two old men in the community approached me to have sex with them. So, I did have sex with them without using a condom. I bought food and clothes for my brothers and sisters and me with the money they gave me. They don't know; they know I am always getting money for food." (Faith)

"I wish I didn't do this thing because I feel dirty inside. I didn't enjoy it because they were rough and smelled terrible. I had sex with them without a condom because then they gave me more money. I was afraid of HIV, but I did have sex with them anyway. I didn't care. When I came home after I had sex with them, I was crying that my life was so low that I must do this. Sometimes, I am glad because I see my family getting food, and they are happy to have it and love me. I love them too." (Faith)

"One man in the community I was having sex with was about 60 years old. If I had sex with him without using a condom, he would always buy me clothes. I like the clothes that he does buy. I have sex with him for R40 (approx. £3)." (Faith)

"When my mother was alive, I was embarrassed. She used to go to the tavern when I was at school. When I came home, she was drunk and shouting at me in the street. I hate that I do feel humiliated. One day, my cousin and I had to go with a wheelbarrow to get her. She had collapsed by the side of the road. I was angry with her because my friends in the street did laugh, and I was humiliated. I hate alcohol." (Faith)

"I liked to talk with my mother before she did leave us. When she is drunk, it's terrible. One day, my younger brother was at home. My mother was boiling water on the primus stove on the side of the kitchen. She was drunk and knocked it over and burned him. He had a skin graft and was in hospital for three weeks. That is why I do hate alcohol. She did leave us when my father died, so we are alone." (Faith)

"All I know is that when my father passed away, no one did take care of me. It was my big sister who did care for us, and she didn't have a job. This made me afraid. I asked myself how we would get food." (Faith's brother).

"My friends did know that my mother did die of AIDS. After my mother passed away, we were poor, and I did get scabies. My friends did say I was also having AIDS, and they did go away from me. So, I sit in the class during a break at school and write poems. I am lonely because they treat me like this." (Faith)

"I had to take care of my brothers and sisters. That is all I did. I knew they must go to school, so I only thought about that." (Faith)

"No one wants us anymore. We are like rubbish that blows around. We go here and there, but no one wants us. We are like a dirty person who is made to be outside, and we want to be loved, but we are rejected. No one can love you like your mother." (Faith)

"I can't talk to my friends about how I feel because I am afraid, they will not understand me, and they will laugh when I tell them how low I feel. So, I just keep it to myself. I feel sad and sometimes cry, but it doesn't make me feel better." (Faith)

"Sometimes I feel like a walking dead person. I have no life in me, just pain. I think if I did kill myself, no one would miss me anyway." (Faith)

"My cousin's sister brought me some clothes at Christmas time. Our clothes were old by that time, and I did have hope that I could go to church again because I did have nice clothes to wear. That made me look to the future and see that it will get better for my brother and sisters and me." (Faith)

"I go every Saturday to my special bible class. There are ten in this class. We study, learn, and discuss things relating to the word of God there. I love my group because we all share and trust them. It's good to belong there. I am strong because of that group. Last year we did go on a camp together. It was too much fun. I love my friends in this group, and they love me, too. We talk about the future in this group, which gives us all hope. Love Jesus too much, and I am learning to trust him." (Faith)

"The morning after my mother's funeral, a neighbour came to my home and brought me food. This gave me hope because he was kind to me." (Faith)

Faith testified that she could forgive, was healed from shame, and felt clean.

Rose

The following week, we went to a home in the middle of the township. I arrived at this home and noticed that the front door was propped closed with a piece of wood. There was a gate to the home that closed, and unusually, the grass of the lawns was green. The young lady, whom I will call Rose, was waiting for us. I brought food, soap, body moisturiser cream, eggs, bread, and a cool drink.

Rose was 14 years old, she let us into the home, and I remember thinking life had simply left this home. The lounge was empty, the windows were broken, and the front door was off its hinges. It was dull and dark. She showed us into her bedroom. The glass in her window was broken, and all the kitchen utensils were in that room. She lived in one room of this home and had a lock on her bedroom door.

She was welcoming and was also keen to tell her story. The story was full of grief; Rose experienced much pain associated with the poverty she was enduring. A Mama in her street was helping her, but there wasn't money for food, shoes, or clothes. Her school uniform was, however, clean. She told us that she liked to sit alone at school and eat her lunch, which one of the teachers brought in for her every day.

She enjoyed being peaceful in a safe place. I remember her telling us that she could feel God in the sunlight, and he was warm. She went to church with a Mama on the street every Sunday and loved scripture and found peace and solace there. She shared her journey of grief with us and how she was beginning to see some hope for the future. She spoke fondly of her parents and was unwilling to leave the home, which was her father's.

Most of all, I learned from Rose the importance of birthdays. She told us how her father used to make her birthday special, buy her presents, make a meal in the evening, and have a birthday cake. Rose spoke about her birthdays being like nothing days; she felt she had just come from the water, and her sense of belonging was broken. She was beginning to find the way forward through the kindness of teachers, her pastor, and the community worker I was with as my translator, whose organisation was supporting Rose with food and assisting with school clothes. Through the GoGo Trust, we were able to fix her windows and door. I always think of Rose when it's someone's birthday and seek to add to making birthdays special. Rose asked us to pray with her before we left, and we encouraged her. I remember her smiling as we left. She felt seen sharing her story and blessed that she knew it would be recorded and helpful for others. When it's your birthday, can you remember Rose and children like Rose? If you are a praying person, pray. She encourages us all to celebrate our birthdays with loved ones and make sure to "Make someone's birthday special and full of celebration".

In her own words

> "Since the death of my mother, I feel like a piece of rubbish tossed about." (Rose)

> "When my father was alive, I always did have hope. He always seemed to get a piece job (casual work), and I was glad because then he got food and paraffin for us. When he died, my hope went. I miss him because he did give me hope." (Rose)

> "By the time my father was alive, many people stayed at my home. It was nice to be together with them all. I loved my father so much because he was kind to me and took care of me. When I played outside with my friends, he sat on the bench and watched me. I like him to do that because I feel important then. After he died, they all went, and my stepmother did also go away. Then, I was alone in the house and had not been alone before that time. I

am scared and lonely. I like to be outside now, not in my home. It's cold now and empty." (Rose)

"When my mother was sick, no one came to help me; at school, no one wanted to play with me, so I sat in the class by myself during break time. I did feel very sad about this, and when I was caring for my mother, I was anxious because I didn't know what is always right to do." (Rose)

"When she was resting in bed, I used to cook and feed her. My mother she did like it when I did feed to her soup. I knew she was dying of AIDS even though she didn't tell me." (Rose)

"On Mother's Day this year at school, my friends are all talking about what they will do on Mother's Day. I did move away from them when they were talking because I didn't have a mother. So, there is nothing I can say. It was horrible in school because the teacher made us all stand up and tell the class what we were doing on Mother's Day. So, I did stand up and say nothing. I cried, and the teacher told me to sit down. I feel pain in me." (Rose)

"When my father was alive, he used to buy me a cake and a present which were usually clothes. Now, when it's my birthday, it's a day of nothing. It's just like that. On that day I focus on my schoolwork. If I think too much, I am sore in my heart." (Rose)

"I just went to my friend's house to eat something this Christmas. I had no presents; I was alone in my home. I listened to the radio then went to him at his home and had a lovely meal. I was glad for that. It was not like that when my father was alive." (Rose)

"When I was at school after my father died, I was worried all the time. I couldn't do my studies because all the time I was thinking, how can I get food and money and who will take care of me?" (Rose)

"The day my father died, my hope died because no one will ever love me like he did. I was close to him in his heart, and now he is gone." (Rose)

"After my father died, I used just to want to be alone. It was like a bad dream to me. I couldn't believe what was happening, and I was very distressed by this." (Rose)

"At school, when my friends talk about their parents, I feel lonely. I have nothing to say because my parents have died. So, I walk away, and I sit by myself. I think about my mother and father, but they are dead now. That makes me to be lonely." (Rose)

"I was hanging the clothes out to dry in the garden, and I did feel like my mother was standing next to me." (Rose)

"I just knew that no one would love to be like my father did, which made me too sad. There were many times I did wish to be dead so that I could be to my father." (Rose)

"I am angry that our grants took so long to come because we are still hungry and do not have enough clothes." (Rose)

"After my mother died, I used just to want to be alone. It was like a bad dream to me. I couldn't believe what was happening, and I was very distressed by this." (Rose)

"Sometimes I feel so low, and I hate myself because since my father did die, I am so poor. I feel so low." (Rose)

"After my father did die and my stepmother did leave me, I was very afraid because I had never stayed alone before. I was scared about who would take care of me. No one wanted me in my family when my father did die, no-one. That did make me to be sad." (Rose)

"The only person that did care for me was my father. After he did die, no one did care. I thought I would kill myself so I can be with him." (Rose)

My friends waited outside my house to walk to school with me after the death of my mother. I was glad because they did show kindness to me." (Rose)

"After the death of my father, I was alone. My teacher saw that I was suffering, and she took me home to be with her every weekend. I was so glad because she was kind to me. She liked me, and that gives me hope." (Rose)

"My friend at school could see I was struggling. So, he came to get me to jog with him every night. It was good to run. I felt free and in my mind. This gave me a good feeling that I had a future." (Rose)

"When I went to my married sister, her husband bought me schoolbooks. That gave me hope because I can stay in school and do my exams. They helped me, and I was glad. No one can make it without help." (Rose)

"I like to go to dancing. I like it, and I pretend I am a princess. It is good for me because when I dance, I forget everything I do and pretend to be a famous dancer. Sometimes, when I dance, I feel like I can do anything in the future, which makes me have hope." (Rose)

"One of the ladies in my community is having a community sewing project. I do go there to be with them. They are like mothers, teaching me how to make mats and clothes. I do like them too much. They help me when I have a problem, which gives me hope. It's a good place for me. I belong there, which makes me feel good in my heart." (Rose)

Rose found hope in the kindness of others and the presence of God. She rediscovered hope because she was helped. When you think of Rose, think of Birthdays, loving your neighbour as yourself, and the words, "I was a Stranger, and you invited me in". Her encouragement makes someone's birthday special.

Sipo

A young man known to the community worker wanted to be interviewed. He stayed in a very overcrowded home at the far end of the township. He was with his extended family but lived in a shack in the garden. It was a clean and tidy shack with a knitted blanket on the bed, which was beautifully made, and his clothes were neatly hanging on coat hangers on the walls. He had a bed, a desk, and a chair in his shack. Let's call him Sipo.

I prepared for this interview, bought bread, chicken, eggs and porridge to give him, and bought cookies and juice to share with him. We arrived at his home and met his family. He signed the informed consent form and said he didn't want to talk to us. His aunt asked if we could pray for the family, which we did, and then we left. I received another call from the community worker about three days after this, who said Sipo wanted to talk to me. So, I prepared for the interview again and went to his home.

We went through the same thing as before, and again, he said he didn't want to talk to us. I knew there was a reason, but I didn't know what. We prayed for the family and left again. The drive to his home was about 40 minutes from my home. A few days later, I was asked to return to Sipo's home and prepare in the same way. I felt peace and knew it was the right thing to try again, so we went. As we arrived at the home, I wasn't sure what to expect but hoped it would be different. He signed the consent form again, came with three glasses and a plate, and wanted to show us his room.

We walked into the backyard and saw his room, and we all sat on benches in the yard away from the home. I thanked him for his time, and he wanted to explain why he had sent us away the previous two times. He said that if we kept a good attitude and returned for a third time, he knew he could trust us. The children were opening their lives with the most challenging and painful things, and I was a stranger. I could communicate that it was a privilege to listen to him. He was a shy boy, but when he smiled, he had a great smile. He was living with two aunts from his mother's family. He loved going to school, church, and playing football. His story was complex. His parents had died of AIDS, and he was left homeless. He slept in a chicken coup in Njoli Square (in the middle of Kwazakhele township) after his mother passed away and was simply distraught. He begged for food and eventually ended up sleeping in a chicken coup in a distant relative's yard with a blanket and a pillow, as there was no room for him in the home. He loved to fall asleep looking at the stars and watching the moon.

Sipo experienced peace sleeping outside and began to regain hope for life and the future. He dreamed of working and owning his own home and knew that God was with him. He had a song he sang; "I know the Lord will make way for me, I know the Lord will make way for me, if I live a holy life shun the wrong and do the right, I know the Lord will make way for me" ... It's a beautiful song which he sang for us. A local community worker found his extended family, and they fostered him, which meant he had a grant (approximately £45 a month). In the household where he was living in a shack in the garden, no one was working. It is impossible to expect family members to provide for nieces and nephews when no one works in the family home. Sipo now had a bedroom of his own, was going to school, doing well at school, and beginning to make friends again. He was learning to trust.

In his own words

> "I used to have my own room when my mother was alive. Since she died, I lived with my aunt. I slept in the lounge after everyone else had gone to bed. I pull two chairs together and sleep like that before I have my shack." (Sipo)

> "On weekends, I do the washing for my cousin and me. I cook, and we clean the house together. If we are struggling, sometimes our friends come and help us clean the house. When my mother was alive, it was not like that. She was doing everything for us. Now we must do it ourselves." (Sipo)

> "When I am not at school, I wash my clothes, clean the house, cook and stay with my friends. I miss having my mother at home. She always cooked and cleaned for us even when she was sick." (Sipo)

> "I do suffer because of my clothes. I feel humiliated. Sometimes I don't look nice because if I need a shirt, I just take a shirt. I iron it and wear it even if it is not nice. Even if my shoe has no sole, I polish it and wear it. What can I do? It's all I have so I must wear it. Sometimes I go to school without shoes. It was not like that when my mother was here because she did have a job ... before she got sick and died." (Sipo)

> "I was worried when my mother did die, all the time I am thinking where I can get another mother? What will I do? Who will take care of us?" (Sipo)

"The worst thing since my grandmother died is that I don't know where I must go to for help. And sometimes I don't know what to do." (Sipo)

"The truth is that even if I can get help from my relatives. I can't tell them because I have no money for travel. And if I get R2.00 I would rather buy bread than make a call to my relatives." (Sipo)

"All I can say is that when my grandmother died it was too much for me. She was too good to me after the death of my mother, and I did love her too much. She did pass away and I did feel like I did die inside my heart." (Sipo)

"All I can say is I did cry and cry. It seemed like it was not happening to me but to someone else. It was too unreal to me that my mother did pass away." (Sipo)

"I knew I had to go on in my life, but I didn't know how to. Sometimes I wanted to go on and sometimes I didn't." (Sipo)

"The worst time to me was when I was sleeping in a rainbow chicken cupboard in Njoli Square where they keep the crates for chickens. I was cold and hungry and dirty. No one cared for me. I was neglected by everyone, even the people who did pass me by on the street." (Sipo)

"The thing that does make me angry is when there is no food in my home. I just burn inside, and I go, and I do walk around I don't want anyone to be close to me. I walk and walk till I calm down. It was not like that when my mother was alive." (Sipo)

"I am angry that no one does take care of us. Sometimes I just want to shout because I am so angry." (Sipo)

"I was overwhelmed when my grandmother did go to my aunt, and they did take all the items in my home. I asked myself how many bad things can happen to a person. I did lose my grandmother, my home, and my family." (Sipo)

"Many times, I didn't know what to do after my father died. I was uncertain even how to buy electricity for the meter." (Sipo).

"All I can say is I know God is there, and he does help me." (Sipo)

"Without my prayer, I would give up. I know God does listen, and a grandmother in the community prays for me every day. This gives me hope for the future." (Sipo)

"Education is my hope, so I go to school and learn. Even if I have a torn trouser or no food, I drink water and go to school. One day, I told my teacher about boys on my street who are not attending school. I ask him to come to talk with them. He did come and tell them about why we are to learn. He likes me too much because I am serious about my studies, which gives me hope in my life." (Sipo)

"I am just playing chequers (a board game) with my friends. I do play all over the weekend under a tree by my house. I do play well, and the community do like it when I do play because I have sneaky moves, and it's cool." (Sipo)

"I am playing hockey at my school. I like to be in a team. I feel like I do belong there. I am important to my team, and they are important to me. It makes me to be glad. They encourage me, and that makes me strong in my heart." (Sipo)

"When I am playing hockey, I am like everyone else. I don't even think about being an AIDS orphan; I just am glad to have a great team to play in." (Sipo)

Sipo told me it is important not to give up. There is light in God, and he shows us this in the strength of the sun, the stars and Jesus. When you think of Sipo, think about trust and hope.

Nelson

Learning to be adaptable became important when undertaking these interviews, and learning to listen and be present was vital. I went through the motions of preparing for another interview, buying eggs, bread, and chicken, and taking in biscuits and juice.

I will call this young man Nelson. Nelson lived with his cousin. We arrived at his home, and he showed us inside. He was keen to talk but had parameters. He wanted to see me write down certain things that he spoke about as well as being recorded. He started to talk to us in his home, but I could sense he wasn't comfortable. He wanted to speak to me but didn't want to look at me and said he was hungry. I remember thinking, what if I interviewed him in my car? I said this to him, and he was happy. So, he got in the back of my car, the interpreter and I sat in the front, and we drove to a place in the township far from his home. We picked up Kentucky on the way. I parked the car, and he began to talk. He could then speak to me in a private space from the back seat without the community's gaze, eat chicken and chips, and not have to look at me. It worked; that's what was important.

His story was full of adversity and grief. He and his cousin used to go to the bush before school to cut sticks and make brooms to sell so they could buy food. Their uncle used to bring food to them until he stopped. They went to find him and found him dead in his home. Nelson was very matter of fact about this.

He recounted to me crimes he committed, which were essentially stealing clothes off people's washing lines to sell them for food. He felt he was a good boy and wanted to be seen as that, but he was worried about his reputation. He clearly articulated his stumbling block. He couldn't believe that Jesus was resurrected from the dead; therefore, he couldn't accept God as his Heavenly Father. It was all very logical to him. After the interview, I explained to him this happened by revelation. He hated being an orphan and feeling he had no place to belong. I asked him to visit his pastor and ask these questions. He was a very insistent young man. He asked for us to pray for him, which we did, and I drove home.

The following week, I received a call from the community worker asking me to buy potato beetroot, spinach, and tomato seeds, which I did. I was also asked to buy bars of soap. I was also asked to purchase ten sets of each packet of seeds. I did and returned to Nelson's home with the community worker. All I can say is he was different. We sat in his lounge. He told me that he woke up a few days ago knowing that Jesus was raised from the dead and that he could become a Christian, which meant to him God was his Heavenly Father and he wasn't an orphan anymore.

He wanted the seeds and soap to give to people in the community he had previously stolen things from and asked if we could also go and buy bread and milk for these people, which we did. He took bread, seeds and soap to everyone concerned off his own back and apologised to everyone he had stolen from. He regained his reputation, which gave him confidence. It was an encouraging story and a most wonderful visit.

In his own words

"After the death of my mother, I was left alone without any money. What can a person do without money? I can't buy clothes, pay school fees, or even buy food. This did distress me too much. Because I had no money, I couldn't eat or wash my clothes. I feel humiliated because of this. One day, I did go to school without shoes because I didn't have any. The children did laugh at me. I knew my education was important, so I went barefoot. Then a teacher from school gave me shoes." (Nelson)

"After my mother died and my grandmother did leave to go to my aunt, I had no money. So, I go to the bush to cut sticks to make brooms. These brooms are for sweeping the house. I sold them, and with that, I bought food. I didn't go to school then. If I did go to school, I have no money for food. So, I do let go of my education to get money to eat food." (Nelson)

"One time, a shopkeeper accused me of stealing from his shop. I went to prison for a month. I didn't do it, but they accuse me because they know I am alone and I am struggling to eat. I didn't do it, and I was sad because prison was too bad for me. In that place, the men do have sex with other men ... I saw it, and I hate that thing; it's too terrible. I never will go back there. I didn't steal but they do blame me anyway because I have no money." (Nelson)

"One time after the death of my mother, I did stop going to school and get a job. I did work in a bakery making bread from 7 in the morning till 11 at night. They pay me 20 Rand (approx. £1.20). I don't want to be a slave, so I left." (Nelson)

"I was a good boy when my grandmother was looking after us. When my relatives did come and take her and all our furniture, I was sad. I had no clothes and food. I did bad things. I used to wait in the street and rob people. I would beat them up and steal anything I could so I could survive. I am ashamed of what I did. I don't do it now because I get help through Sisonke Sophumelela (Orphan Care Programme). Now I am in school and have a uniform, clothes, and enough food to eat." (Nelson)

"I went to jail for a month for something I didn't do. I just got blamed because people know I am doing wrong things in the community. In jail, it was terrible. I was beaten, and all the men in my cell were having sex with one another. I was not raped, but the guy next to me was. It was too terrible. I am never going back there again." (Nelson)

"I felt such pain after the death of my mother. I didn't even want to be with my friends. All I want is to be alone. So, in the break time at school, I just sat by myself." (Nelson)

"The day my mother passed away was too terrible. I did just come home and sit. I didn't know what to do. I just sat. I didn't know what to do!" (Nelson)

"I couldn't believe what had happened to me. One day, I was taken care of. The next day, I was left without any food. It was like that I was just abandoned. There was no one to take care of me. I was alone." (Nelson).

"My grandmother was taking care of us after my mother did pass away. She is making food for us and boiling water so we can wash. She is dead now, and my home is a lonely place without her care." (Nelson)

"I did go to a support group for orphans in our community that did help me too much because I see others are also suffering like me." (Nelson).

"I get angry when I see my friends in new school clothes, and I have holes in my shoes that do make me angry." (Nelson)

"I didn't think a person's life can change so much. After my mother died, I was overwhelmed because every day was difficult for me. I didn't know where to get food, how to wash my clothes, and how to cook. I cried too much I wanted to die." (Nelson)

"I went to my aunt to get help. She sent me away, and I didn't know what to do. I went to the bush. I just sat there, and I cried." (Nelson)

"Everything was too much when my mother did die. I was sad all the time. My life is too difficult now because no one is taking care of me and my brother. This makes me be crushed in my heart." (Nelson)

"When I thought about the future, I was unsure what would happen to me. Everything changed. I was now alone, and I had no money, no job, and no one to take care of me." (Nelson)

"After the death of my mother, I just wanted to die. The pain in my heart was too bad, and I didn't want to live." (Nelson)

"If my grandmother's sister didn't stay to take care of us after the death of my grandmother, I don't know what we would have done. We had no money, and we had no food. My grandmother's sister does use her pension to take care of us. She cares for us, and I hope for the future." (Nelson)

"The greatest thing that happened to me was when my uncle came and paid for me to go to the bush so I could become a man. This gave me much hope that I could be a man, not an old boy. I did feel after this I had a future, which gave me much hope." (Nelson)

"The minister of my church said that God is near to the broken-hearted and collects our tears. So, I think when I cry, God is catching my tears in his hand, which gives me hope because when I cry, it means something." (Nelson)

"When I play soccer, it is like I am free to be anything. We are champions in the community. We win everything we play, and that makes me feel glad. Even if we lose, I don't mind as long as it's a good game." (Nelson)

"I play soccer for a team in the community. I love it; it makes me feel good. My friends shout my name when I do play and encourage me. I am a defender and play well, so it is good for me. Playing soccer makes me hope that one day I will get a good job and be successful, just like when I play soccer." (Nelson)

When I think of Nelson, I think of redemption and the impossible becoming possible. I think he would say there is a God who is a Heavenly Father, and He answers prayers.

On another visit we undertook, I visited children who didn't have a bed; instead, they slept on a blanket on the bare springs of a mattress frame. We sat on upturned buckets in this home as our seats. It was a cold day. There was nothing kind in the environment in which they lived. The home was poor. There was little food in the house, and the children spoke of the trauma they experienced on losing their Mum to AIDS. They were living with their uncle, a thin man with a warm smile. The children felt safe with him but had no means to care for them. The interpreter I was with called a social worker whom she knew and this family was helped. We went and bought enough food for this family for a week. We organised money for a mattress, sleeping bags, and pillows for the children. They already had blankets. I was so grateful the interpreter knew who to contact. There was love in this home but no money to buy food.

When I think of these two children, I will call them Yolander and Nobuthembu, children just need to be cared for and loved.

Once the interviews were completed, I transcribed them verbatim. Of course, I did this in the luxury of my own home. This felt strange, as the voices I listened to were familiar, as were the stories. The window I looked out from was onto a lovely garden with Bougainvillea growing outside. I could eat fresh, cold fruit from the fridge and drink cold, clean water from the tap. I felt conflicted.

The day came when all these interviews were transcribed and printed onto crisp white paper. I hand-delivered these to my professor. I stopped at the coffee shop overlooking the beach on my way home. Approximately 750,000 people live in the township communities in Gqeberha. I had interviewed eight children in total, but I couldn't help but wonder how many stories were similar to the ones I had listened to (8).

Chapter 7
Pulling Together What Was Said

"There is no blue without yellow and orange."
– Vincent Van Gogh

Who knew it would be so hard to hear the words of these children? I know we live in a time where we access information quickly and maybe don't give credence to the things we perhaps should do. Visiting the children and listening to their stories was very humbling. They wanted their stories to be told as this seemed to give some meaning to their suffering. These children verbalised feelings of being distressed, helpless, abandoned, lonely, and grief-stricken.

At a time when they should be cared for, these children found themselves discarded because the burden of caring for them in existing family structures was too great. Extended family members who were supposed to care for them were already overburdened by poverty, unemployment, and decay in their family structures because of HIV/AIDS. There was no one to take them in and care for them. They became bewildered, confused, and hurt and found it difficult to describe the enormity of the devastation they experienced. They became like fledglings thrown from the nest without a safe place to land. They were overwhelmed and devastated by their experience. Children missed their parents when they died. They also sometimes expressed relief when they were freed from the responsibility of caring for their parent who was dying of AIDS. They lived emotionally conflicted.

"Ikhaya" is the Xhosa word for home, a place of security, care, warmth, love, affection, and belonging, but following the death of a parent or loved one, it becomes a place of challenge where children who have become orphans were ill-equipped to care for themselves. How can they feed themselves when they have no money to buy food? How can they cook when the relatives came and took away the cooker and the fridge? How can they wash their clothes without money to buy soap? Home became barren as if the very life of a home once known had seeped away through the walls. Bewildered and alone without money, the orphans must adapt to feed and clothe themselves. They missed their mother, father, or loved one who used to care for them, and they needed to survive. Children missed having their parents or loved ones express care on special days. Children missed feeling a sense of belonging. Most orphans have fallen through the net of care that has traditionally come from the extended family through "ubuntu". Ubuntu has been translated as "humaneness" and is derived from the expression umumtu ngumuntu ngabantu (a person is a person because of others/a person can only be a person through others) (9).

Children became overwhelmed by a lack of finances. The reduction of household income following the death of a parent or carer must not be an excuse for education providers to exclude orphans from school, but this did occur. Orphaned girls were particularly vulnerable to sexual abuse and prostitution because they had assumed adult responsibilities such as caring for their dying parents and raising their siblings; they were in a state of panic as they had been left abandoned by their extended family and were without any means of financial support

They were bewildered by their overwhelming circumstances and did turn to prostitution to earn money to meet the basic needs of their family (8).

Abuse, rejection, betrayal, disappointment, judgment, criticism, and grief caused pain in their lives. It has been stated that emotional pain is often more devastating than physical pain. "Medication can be taken for physical pain, but emotional pain is not easy to deal with" (8). When pain and discomfort become more than people can withstand, they turn to a substance to alleviate the pain they feel (8). It was for this alleviation of emotional pain that the orphans smoked dagga as it made them forget the horror of their situation and feel peaceful and carefree.

The children all described the feelings and emotions they experienced due to the devastation of becoming AIDS orphans. They used words such as "bewildered, distressed, and in pain". They were, at times, very articulate and willing to describe their feelings associated with their experiences and painted in words a picture that detailed the feelings and emotions they experienced on becoming AIDS orphans.

All the children mentioned being abandoned by their extended family at their greatest time of need; they were left to care for themselves without adequate resources. The feeling of being abandoned was acute, and the children I interviewed said that they wanted to "die" because they "felt too bad".

The children expressed feelings of being lonely because of the loss of their parent or loved one, the rejection of family members, and because of the ridicule they faced at school and in the community from friends. They felt ridiculed because they had become poor and because their parent or loved ones had died of AIDS or AIDS-related illnesses. This led to friends at school spreading false rumours about the orphans that they, too, were infected with HIV and would die. The orphans responded by withdrawing themselves from these relationships, causing them to become the "odd one out". They experienced loneliness as they isolated themselves by staying home over the weekends, walking to school alone, and spending their break time sitting in the classroom alone.

All the children were "thrown to the wind" and tossed around greatly by their devastating circumstances. Their lives were void of help. They became like saplings trying to root in harsh, dry soil. They were desperate to survive despite being crushed because of being disregarded.

Anger is a compelling emotion. It is experienced when a person is extremely displeased, irritated, frustrated, or enraged by the injustice of some sort; it is to experience animosity towards, resentment, or have a bad temper towards another person or object. Anger can be described as swelling with rage or becoming exasperated by injustice and violation, a sense of feeling one's blood rising and feeling mad, very mad, and becoming incensed by an event, causing the reaction of being in a huff and pushing others away. All the children experienced anger on becoming AIDS orphans. They expressed at times that they became irrational and before the death of their parent or loved one that they had been "good children".

The children further described feeling overwhelmed by their life circumstances after becoming orphans. They experience intense emotions because of the loss of their parent or loved one and the complicated circumstances they find themselves in because of the financial insufficiency they experience. The financial hardship experienced by these orphans often led to multiple losses. i.e. loss of status, loss of schooling, loss of any more new clothes, loss of food and shelter and the loss of belonging to a family. They were bewildered, shocked and overwhelmed by the hardship they faced and the intense grief emotions they felt. The world as they knew it has changed, and they are overwhelmed by the enormity of their new reality.

Following the death of their parent or loved one, the children were all uncertain because their lives as they knew them had changed beyond recognition. They were uncertain regarding the future. How will we survive? How will I continue to go to school? How will I eat? All became commonplace questions to answer. The known was replaced by the unknown. Uncharted waters were ahead; they were full of uncertainty, insecurity and doubt.

Their lives, in the first instance, had become devoid of all hope and full of pain. They suffered loss, rejection, abandonment, and despair. Some of the orphans quite simply hated being orphans. They felt humiliated, as if in some way it was their fault, and felt low and unloved. Some said that they wanted to be free of pain, and others wanted to die so that they, too, could be with their loved ones. They were ashamed of the poverty that had come upon them on the death of their parent or loved one and hated being hungry and cold.

Hope

However, in the middle of this overwhelming poverty, grief, and isolation, they did rediscover hope to go on living, but this was usually linked to an intervention. This intervention was centred around kindness, generosity or finding endless hope in God and Jesus.

The children relied on relationships to restore hope. Hope was fragile initially as the orphans found it difficult to accept and trust the help offered to them through their relationships with friends, boyfriends, and girlfriends or through their local church community. Hope was restored through the demonstration of care through practical giving.

They began to trust people who reached out and offered practical support. Such as a pastor visiting them and offering to pray, teachers bringing a packed lunch to school so they could eat lunch or clinic sisters giving children, money for food or taxi fare. Pastors visit and pray for them, and teachers bring them lunch and school uniforms. Clinic sisters give them money for food and taxi fare. They loved the sense of belonging they experienced in playing football, playing with their friends, attending sewing groups, and attending church. They loved it when their friends were kind, generous and thoughtful towards them. They loved it when they could begin to do life with others again, not separated or isolated but in a place of togetherness.

There was a paradox that the children experienced in their relationships with their extended families following the death of their loved ones. In one instance, the extended family came to the homes of the orphans and took household items following the death of their parent or loved one and failed to give adequate support, while in another instance, the extended family members offered help in the form of practical support, which benefited the children and helped them to regain hope.

All the children referred to God and shared experiences of praying and attending church. The children called to God in distress, and many searched for the truth about God. They had questions to be answered and were all seeking comfort and hope. What was apparent was that they felt hope when they prayed. Hope seemed to be awakened in them when they participated in activities that they enjoyed and were good at, like football.

> The children stressed the importance of their education. They enjoyed the school environment because they were not treated differently from other students, and they all enjoyed not feeling different from their peers. They were motivated to learn and keen to show me and the community worker their schoolwork. They all spoke about becoming doctors, lawyers, engineers, teachers, social workers and plumbers. Their dreams of a future were alive and fuelled by their ability to learn and do well in school tests and be recognised by their teachers.

> The school environment is the friendliest of all the environments these children embrace, which is why they attend school. They go to school because they aren't different there; they are simply children who

need a good education to equip them for the future. Going to school gave these children hope.

They were glad to talk about the community groups to which they belonged and the activities they participated in in these groups. Belonging to community groups made the orphans forget their problems and gave them a space to belong. They all enjoyed the groups they were involved in and felt strengthened emotionally through being involved in the community activities they pursued. The children loved playing games. They loved being a part of a team, and they loved to win. All the children interviewed explained that playing sports in the community gave them a sense of belonging and enabled them to be fully involved in an activity without thinking about their problems. They loved participating and supporting a team. This made them feel glad (8).

Chapter 8
Sisonke Sophumelela and Julian's Children

"Some painters transform the sun into a yellow spot; others transform a yellow spot into the sun."
– Picasso

Sisonke Sophumelela in Xhosa means "Together we can overcome". I wondered if bringing these children together would be good for them. The community worker, whom I will call Noxolo, visited Faith, Rose, Nelson, Sipo, and Atenkosi and asked if they would like to meet in a private place with each other. They said they would like to. At this time, more money came into the GoGo Trust, and we could commit to buying monthly groceries for these child-headed household families, paying electricity money so the children could cook and study, and paying Noxolo to visit the children, take the groceries and meet with the children once a month as a group. The poverty these children endured was overwhelming, and they needed immediate help, which we were able to get to them. My Master's was completed at this stage, but another journey was beginning.

Our First Meeting

Noxolo gave taxi fares (taxis in this context means a small minibus) to the children to meet us at Vukukhanye Pre-school in Kwazakhele, and we had our first meeting there in the evening. I bought cooked sausages, hot chocolate, bread, and ketchup. We made "Hot Dogs" ... who knew teenagers could eat so much!!!! ... so, this is how we began. I opened in prayer and was invited by Nelson to read a scripture, which I did. Nelson thanked me, and then he started to share. Then, all the children shared what they wanted to do. They spoke in Xhosa. I was merely an observer and didn't require translation. The children were animated. Some cried, others sat. They thanked us for bringing them together, and they decided their group should have a name, so they called it Sisonke Sophumelela. which means "Together we can overcome". We were all on a journey together. The children were beginning to overcome by seeing themselves in the stories of others and were grateful. I was asked to close this meeting in prayer, which I did. It was their group.

It was a wonderful encouragement to have things put in my hands at the right time. A friend who was a social worker in South Africa made me aware of a curriculum specifically developed to help these vulnerable children through developing support groups. It was centred around the following concepts: "I am, I can, and I have". The course for this curriculum was in Pietermaritzburg (approximately ten hours' drive by coach from Port Elizabeth). I arrived by coach and drove home to Port Elizabeth through the Transkei. It was a beautiful part of South Africa. When I returned to Port Elizabeth, Noxolo and I spent the day in a nice restaurant going through this support group curriculum. Noxolo resonated with the key aspects and was keen to implement it with the children who attended Sisonke Sophumelela. I thought the children should decide. Cultural differences can sometimes be challenging, but we worked this through and came to a compromise. Noxolo introduced the course to the children; they told us it made them feel special that something was written to help them. By this time, I had read the course three times and found it helpful, intuitive, and encouraging. I was relieved that it was written to meet their unique needs. The children were beginning to feel seen and understood and not alone. This was life-giving for them.

The children loved the home visits; they were reassured that someone was coming to their home to listen to them and bring food. Food insecurity causes desperate anxiety. Knowing now they would be given food regularly brought relief and helped them focus on their school studies. All the children attended school, and some started attending their local churches. I observed during the initial Sisonke Sophumelela meetings and would bring refreshments and pray as I was invited. It was a private space (dare I even say it became a holy place) where profound challenges and complex grief were shared and understood. The children found their voices, and their hearts began to heal. They found purpose and life and began discussing the future, remembering and valuing what their parents had taught them.

There was, however, anxiety around me going into the townships in the dark. We initially had these meetings in the early evening. The sun sets early evening, regardless of the time of year, between 6pm and 7.30pm. The children also asked if we could meet on a Saturday instead. So, we began to do that. It was safer and easier for us all.

I had been praying for the children and was drawn to a certain activity in the program we were beginning to implement. It involved writing a note, putting it in a balloon, and letting it float into the sky. The idea was to let something go. I demonstrated this to the children, who thought it was a great idea. So, we sat in our room, Nelson asked me to pray, and the children began writing notes. Some asked for more than one balloon. Nelson wrote three notes and put them in his balloon. We tied the balloons with some challenge, and then the children held their balloons. The children wanted to pray, so they all prayed. Then we stood outside and let the balloons fly. The joy I experienced at that moment surprised me, and I think the children were, too. As we went inside, Nelson prayed for us all. We then ate lunch together and went home.

Our meetings continued, as did the home visits. After this time, I began to see a newfound confidence and openness in the children. I saw the children continue to move from grief, hopelessness, fear and sadness into a place of hope and speaking about the future. They were all doing well at school and were good at keeping themselves safe.

One lovely memory I will share is when we took all the children away on a farm near Addo, just north of Port Elizabeth. A friend of mine, Tony, a retired teacher, organised camps for young people to teach them leadership. We arrived at the farm, and the children sat around the fire, cooking meat and talking. They had become a tight-knit group. I sat with them for a while, and they started singing. It was beautiful to watch them together, away from the township, having fun. We all slept in tents that night under a beautiful African sky. I was up early in the morning and sat around the fire embers from the night before. Sipo came and sat next to me. He told me of the night he wanted to die and now boldly said his Mum would be so proud of him for completing his studies, and that day, he had learned to count from one to ten in Japanese. He now felt he could achieve anything. Tony, my friend who led the camp, said he had never had such an attentive group of children. They were kind, respectful, and polite. They engaged in confidence-building activities and had a lot of fun. Somehow, they talked me into partaking in the adventure course, which included crawling through the mud on my tummy. The children laughed, I laughed, and I loved it; we all learnt together anything was possible. These children were learning to have fun and be free, and I was learning to trust so we could continue to give financially and help this group of remarkable children complete their school education.

Julian's Children

As the children completed their education and migrated to work, Sisonke Sophumelela became Julian's Children's Orphan Care program. Julian's Children is centred around home visits undertaken by Mtutuzeli and Lungiswa, and essential food items are delivered to these families monthly. This intervention stabilises the home by ensuring food security and enabling the children to remain in school and complete their education. Our children have completed their Grade 12 education (like completing A levels in the UK). They became orphans, experienced much grief, and yet have and are completing their education. Julian's Children is bringing hope. We deliver monthly rice, flour, oil, salt, sugar, samp (coarsely ground corn), beans, washing powder, and porridge. The income available in their homes is mainly through government grants and the government pension so the grandmothers can buy vegetables and meat and pay for other necessities such as travel to work and school uniforms.

As I write this, a young man called Luphelo has completed two years of mechanical engineering. He is a shy but disciplined young man who is either helping with chores in his home, playing football with his friends, going to church, or studying.

Ayabonga has completed his Grade 12 education and is studying to become a chef. He works in an Air B&B and is a delightful, faithful young man committed to his grandmother, uncle, and sister. All the other children we support are in school and doing well. Many want to become social workers as they now have stories of hope and feel they can help others.

For 18 years, the GoGo Trust has been visiting orphans and providing food to children who live in granny-headed households in Kwazakhele and surrounding township communities in Gqeberha. I have come to know in this place that we give what we do, and somehow, this is multiplied into hope and purpose. The children thrive and find purpose in a challenging environment but know much hope and love. They grow in their faith and purpose as they worship and pray and keep doing well at school.

Chapter 9
A Remarkable Man

"How lovely yellow is it stands for the Sun."
– Vincent Van Gogh

Mr Mtutuzeli Beyi

Mtutuzeli in Xhosa means "comforter". When I first met Mtutuzeli, he wore an orange tee shirt and accompanied his sister Lulama to a Tuesday meeting. At this meeting, he shared scriptures with the Mamas. I remember thinking at the time, would he perhaps help me? I was overseeing the Tuesday meetings of the soup cells and Sisonke Sophumelela, Vukukhanye pre-school, as well as writing my master's degree. I wanted to appoint a leader but was unsure how to do so.

Mtutuzeli arranged for me to meet with a group of ladies he knew in New Brighton, a township bordering Kwazakhele. Mtutuzeli asked me to take bread and juice so we could have communion with the Mamas in New Brighton. I arrived at a church with our visitors and met another group of ladies. His recollection of this meeting was that my theology was off as I used brown bread to celebrate communion. He didn't tell me this until sometime later.

He had been working as a volunteer for Isandler, a community group in New Brighton Township. He kept coming to the Tuesday Group and began speaking to the ladies and sharing encouraging words. They appreciated his strength and wisdom, and I asked if he would like to visit the soup cells with me. The GoGo Trust began to pay him at this point. He took on the leadership role of the Tuesday meetings, and the soup cells and my role became more supportive. He stepped into this role and was remarkable. He is kind, dependable, and full of encouragement. His presence and words bring comfort, strength, and hope.

He completed a theology training course, which he loved, and a micro-management and business administration course called a micro-MBA. He is a natural leader; the Mamas and I trusted him. The soup cells became an organisation that Mtutuzeli still leads. He has done extraordinarily well, which is a testimony to his character and consistent faithfulness. He married Lungiswa, a beautiful Xhosa lady who was also full of faith and dignity. She helps him oversee the soup cells, and they visit Julian's Children.

They live in Kwazakhele township. He is a comforter in his community. He visits the soup cells, takes the Tuesday meetings, visits all of Julian's Children every month, and is a friend to many, including me. He is remarkably faithful and kind. Before he was married, he cared for his sister Lulama and her grandchildren. He is a respected uncle to Ayabonga and Mangaliso. He is a safe person for the Mamas and Julian's Children, alongside his wise, beautiful, and kind wife, Lungiswa.

His life is marked by prayer and serving widows, orphans, and other community members. I asked him what he wanted me to tell you when writing this part of the book. He said, "The GoGo Trust is doing good work, which I am proud of. The children are in school as they have hope and pass their exams. The soup cells bring so much hope. The Mamas are bringing much hope and food to hungry people. The poverty in Kwazakhele has been bad since COVID-19. My main testimony is that when we pray, people find jobs, and the word of God brings life, hope, and much healing. The soup is good, and it nourishes hungry people. It's good that we can help. But the hope our community finds in Jesus and his work is wonderful. My home with Lungiswa is a place of goodness for the community. I miss that Sharron is in the UK, but I am glad she gave me the space to become a leader."

I have recently returned from a trip to South Africa to visit Mtutuzeli, our soup cells, and Julian's Children. I took two visitors from the UK with me, Diana and Carol, they wanted to come. Diana is a friend from my church, and Carol is her friend, so we are all friends now. We would pick up some coffee and bread in the mornings and drive into the townships. We took Chakalaka bread (delicious bread) with us for Mtutuzeli. We arrived at his home to pick him up to visit Mama Mandisa's Soup Cell. Diana gave him the bread, for which he was grateful. He put it in his bag for later and said he would save it to have with his wife after the meeting. I've learned much from Mtutuzeli. He is wise, discerning, and true. He stands his ground well and is respected in the community.

He wears a suit when visiting the soup cells and Julian's Children. Another memory of him is when he started working with me, and the GoGo Trust paid him. He had two suits made, complete with waistcoats, so that he could be smart even in hot weather. He is a remarkable man.

I live in London now, and when he is visiting the soup cells and Julian's Children, I receive WhatsApp messages from him with pictures and comments from the Mamas and Julian's Children during the home visits and from the soup cells. I love receiving these messages. When I am in South Africa, Mtutuzeli, Lungiswa and I like to have lunch at Angelos (a restaurant by the sea) and share heart and life. He grew up in apartheid South Africa and was disadvantaged in so many ways. He has transitioned to become a leader, and I am proud to call him my friend.

In honour of our visit last year, he painted his house. He is a dignified, honourable, respected man doing good work in challenging circumstances.

COVID-19

When the COVID-19 pandemic came, it hit the UK more ferociously than South Africa in the first instance. Then, I received a call from Mtutuzeli about the South African government's social isolation measures. He was desperate to keep the soup cells running as many domestic workers living in the townships lost their jobs because of the restrictions imposed. I just wanted him, Lungiswa, their families, the Mamas, and the children to stay well. In the townships, people don't often have freezers or big fridges, and their houses are small, so they need to go food shopping frequently, which means mixing with other people. I looked through the South African government restrictions, and we devised a way of keeping the soup cells running during this time, enabling home visits, and delivering food parcels to Julian's Children while observing these rules. I gave Mtutuzeli a crash course in infection control over a WhatsApp video call. We provided hand gel, face masks, and vitamins to boost the immune systems of the mamas, children, Mtutuzeli, and Lungiswa.

Soup was served using social distancing measures, and our children received their home visits, albeit in the yards of their homes, observing social distancing measures. Mtutuzeli set the AC on his car to internal circulation mode. We prayed Psalm 91 daily and observed good infection control procedures. Mtutuzeli and Lungiswa became proficient in this. The vaccine development and rollout were unknown in South Africa at this time. I remember the day Mtutuzeli received his vaccine, and I was so relieved and grateful. It was about six months after I had received mine in the UK.

The children continued to attend school as online learning wasn't possible in the township communities. The schools separated their pupils into morning and afternoon school, which was cleaned between morning and afternoon school. In this way, the number of children attending the schools at any time was halved. This made social distancing more feasible. The same was true for the supermarkets. Online shopping wasn't possible in these communities, so strict social distancing was observed in queues and the shops. The soup cells became a lifeline during this time, and many people were fed nutritious and delicious soup and encouraged by reading the scripture and praying.

Chapter 10
Sewing Machines

"There is nothing in the world that is not mysterious, but the mystery is more evident in certain things than in others: in the sea, in the eyes of the elders, in the colour yellow, and in music."

– Jorge Luis Borges

The Mamas loved to sew and do beadwork. Mama Evelyn and Tata Simon made many bead items I sold in the UK during my trips home, as the local bead market was saturated. Tata Simon made crocodile beaded key rings from fishing wire and beads. Tata Simon was a wise man. He spent his days growing vegetables and making beaded crocodile key rings in his large garden. Local school children came to Tata's home and learnt to make these keyrings as part of an outreach program through a local school.

The ladies, all apt seamstresses, could sew intricate details of traditional Xhosa dresses and make aprons and school shirts for their children. They prayed for sewing machines to start sewing projects, and I thought we would need about 60 sewing machines. There was also a need for gardening kits and kits to repair cars. This was going to be expensive.

I can't remember exactly how, but I met John Fowler in Port Elizabeth, who worked for Tools with a Mission (TWAM). When I was home in the UK, I drove to Colchester and met with him and his team. We had to agree to pay the customs charges, and they would ship sewing machines, gardening kits and car maintenance kits to South Africa. The container would be delivered to Umtata, and we would have to drive and collect everything in a van. It sounded like an answer to the prayers of the Mamas and an adventure. It was agreed we could have more than I asked for as I was aware of another organisation in Port Elizabeth at Kleinskool that could also benefit.

On returning to South Africa, I said nothing until we knew the container had arrived, and we had a date to drive to Umtata to pick up everything TWAM gave us. My friends Boet, Anikee and Nicky drove for eight hours through the Transkei to Umtata. We collected everything, which filled a small lorry and the back of my truck. We packed everything securely overnight and drove back to Port Elizabeth the following morning.

We took everything to Kleinskool, where a group of young men unloaded everything with us. This equipment was very heavy. Over the next week, I would drive to Kleinskool, fill up my truck with sewing machines, gardening kits, and car repair kits, and deliver them to the soup cells throughout Kwazakhele. These were significant days when many small projects in these communities began with sewing machines, car repair kits and gardening kits.

Whenever I arrived at a soup cell, I unloaded all the goods with help. I had developed a lot of physical strength while working in the township and could carry a 25kg bag of soup powder without help. We unloaded these goods into the garages attached to the soup cells. These goods were delivered to the Mama's homes, and community members would stand in a circle, hold hands, and pray. These resources were received with thanksgiving as if they had come directly from heaven. It was humbling. They were tools with a mission to benefit the community.

Each sewing group was set up as a collective. The GoGo Trust paid the initial amount to purchase needles, material thread, and pins; the sewing proceeds were put into a post office account held by the sewing groups. Money was saved to buy new material, and then in December of each year, the profit was shared between the sewing group members. It worked, and I was astonished. The ladies made me a beautiful Xhosa skirt and a pinafore made from Tata Mandella's material. It's a gorgeous blue.

Chapter 11
Julian's Children

"The joy is an absurd yellow tulip, popping up in my life, contradicting all the evidence that it should not be there."
– Marya Hornbacher

Sisonke Sophumelela became Julian's Children's orphan care branch of the work of the GoGo Trust. I remember driving in South Africa when I stopped at a traffic light. What does the name Julian mean? It means young at heart. I wanted the children we supported to remain young at heart, so I was moved to call our orphan care program Julian's Children, as I have described previously. I have permission from Luyanda and Ayabonga to present their stories to you.

I met Luyanda when he was 16 years old. His Mum died of AIDS, and he felt angry and he also felt shame. He became impoverished very quickly as money left the home. He went to school and loved to learn, but he had no food at home and was very sad. He has always felt things deeply and is expressive in his language use. His Mum impressed upon him the importance of his education, and he continued attending school, completing his Grade 12 education.

He migrated into the workplace with some challenges, but he became responsible. I recently travelled to South Africa to celebrate 20 years of the work of the GoGo Trust. He is now an accomplished young man. He moved forward even when he felt hopeless. Luyanda means "something that continues or loves". He continues, and he still loves. He told me, "The GoGo Trust gave me hope when I had no hope. I knew that someone cared, and I knew I had food to eat. I could go forward because of this, and I am grateful."

Ayabonga means "grateful" in Xhosa. During this same trip, Carol, Diana and I visited Ayabonga at his home. We took a cookery book for him as a gift. He was so thrilled he wrapped his arms around it, hugged it, and said, "I will read this whole book. I will even sleep with it in my bed". He was supported through school by Julian's Children and completed his Grade 12 education. He is a keen rugby player who loves attending church and cooking. He studies at college and works in an Air B & B to learn how to care for tourists. He has a beautiful faith and always prays for us when we visit. He also sings beautifully. He is Lulama's grandson. Her daughter died of AIDS, and Lulama was still relatively young. Lulama wasn't of a pensionable age when she was responsible for caring for her grandchildren, and Mtutuzeli supported the family. The family has been supported by Julian's Children for the last ten years. Lulama now receives her government pension; she sews and visits soup cells. Her home is loving, prayer-filled, full of joy, hope and worship. From their home's stoop (front veranda) is a lovely view across the roofs of the houses in their part of the township. I've seen many beautiful sunsets across those roofs.

A time of change for change

Mtutuzeli led the soup cells, and Julian's Children were all doing well. We both sensed a time of change. Mtutuzeli needed the space to lead with support. I knew it but wasn't sure what that would look like. By this time, I had worked almost daily in the townships for seven years. I was tired but not discouraged. Professor Kotze at NMU told me I was obliged to do a PhD. This felt insurmountable to me. I felt deeply that my roots were being loosened and that I would move back home to the UK. This raised many questions and wasn't without complexity.

One morning, I woke up early. I used to go to a monastery near Grahamstown to have time to pray and reflect. In the morning, I went to the chapel to pray with the brothers. I took a notepad and began to write the outline for a PhD study. I spoke to people I respected and trusted about this, and they felt it was the right next step. I then made an appointment with my professor, and we began to plan what this could look like. It would be a huge undertaking, of that I was aware. This was a challenging time; I was going home. I felt relief on many levels and was excited about creating something that could help children who are living as AIDS orphans in township communities. I was excited to see the seasons and go home and enjoy a Sunday roast in a pub. I had missed being at home and living out of my own culture since first going to South Africa in 1998, which had been both a privilege and a challenge; if I am honest, I felt tired.

So, a new journey began. I spent a year writing a research proposal, preparing documents for ethical approval at the NMU in South Africa, and reading about other researchers' work. It was also arduous but exciting, and I began thinking differently. I was very grateful for being able to take short trips to South Africa during this time and grew in confidence that the day-to-day work of the GoGo Trust was in safe hands. Mtutuzeli, the Mamas and children consistently amazed me. I started reading South African Policy documents to understand the South African government's legislative and policy frameworks and intent to care for orphans and vulnerable children in their nation.

The legislative and policy framework was dense, comprehensive, well-written, and informative. The Bill of Rights is written comprehensively in section 28 of the South African constitution and is in line with articles in the Convention of the Rights of the Child, ratified in South Africa on June 16, 1995. However, the regional policies, although comprehensive in demonstrating intent, fall short in implementation details.

Finally, I began to see a gap. I spent a year reading and writing about legislative policy frameworks concerning children's rights in South Africa (12,13). I remember going for a walk to think and pray. I sat on a seat overlooking the town of Horsham. The thought was simply: who has responsibility in the townships to provide immediate care for children when they become AIDS orphans and are living in the township communities?

In this instance, government employees are primary healthcare nurses, social workers, and psychologists. Could it be that simple? To find out their experiences of providing care and support to children living as AIDS orphans in these communities and ask them what recommendations they would make to improve care and support to meet the unique needs of these vulnerable children, perhaps it was.

I had another meeting with my professor on a subsequent trip to South Africa. We agreed this was the way to progress, so I went through another round of writing documents for the ethics committees at the NMU, the officials in the Department of Health and Social Development, and then the managers in these departments before I could proceed with this study. During this time, I read a lot about how to analyse qualitative data and many examples from other researchers who had already walked this well-trodden path. I struggled at times with the isolation, but there is only one way to write: to be alone. I bought many candles and was sometimes grateful for the company of some four-legged friends. Faithfulness was my only goal: to be faithful to the task and write as well as possible.

Approval letters began to arrive, so I went to South Africa to identify participants who could be part of this study. I drove a lot during this time and had many meetings with government officials and managers in the Department of Health and Social Development. This time, I had many interviews to undertake. The day came when I started to interview primary health care nurses, social workers, and psychologists employed by the South African government to provide care and support to these AIDS orphans. It was an honour to meet these professionals. I met and listened to their experiences of caring for children living in township communities in South Africa and heard the recommendations they wanted to make to improve care and support for these children.

I spent three months driving into the townships, often to remote places, to interview these wonderful people. I then went home, uploaded these interviews onto three devices, and continued until I reached data saturation. That is the point that these professionals were no longer saying anything new. The day before I was due to fly home, I was contacted by a psychologist who wanted to speak to me. So, I took another drive into the township, interviewed this psychologist, drove home, uploaded the interview and returned the recording device to the university. I now had over 20 interviews uploaded which needed to be transcribed. This was a job for when I returned home.

I was physically exhausted at this point, and when I got on the plane from Jo'burg to London, I remember fastening my seat belt and sleeping. I must have heard the plane take off, but I don't recall this. The air steward woke me to ensure I was ok, and I remember eating chicken before sleeping again. It was good to be home in the UK. I left winter in South Africa to enjoy the summer in the UK, which I have always found beautiful. I missed Mtutuzeli, Lulama, the Mamas and the children, and I missed driving into the township communities.

I spent the next year transcribing the interviews, analysing the data, and hopefully, giving credence to the experiences and recommendations made for improving care and support for children living as AIDS orphans in township communities in South Africa. It was sometimes arduous, but being faithful was more important than being successful.

I have always been encouraged by the work of Heidi and Rowland Baker and read all their books. Mama Heidi was speaking at a church meeting in London, and I went to hear her. By this time, I'd written the results of my PhD and now needed to develop a conceptual framework and strategies using the data collected and analysed data. My mind sometimes got tired because of all the thinking, and I had this gremlin I was consistently fighting: you won't finish, Sharron; how can you possibly make a difference? You can't do this. I also found isolation to be a challenge. I sometimes felt I was stagnating, and everyone else's life was moving forward. I spent my days reading, writing, thinking, and trying to be creative. Who was I trying to fool that I could get this PhD over the line? I needed some fresh inspiration to enable me to live well in this space.

That night, listening to Heidi Baker, I was, of course, inspired. She spoke about love. It was beautiful, heaven-sent, and profoundly moving to hear her. She had an altar call, at which point I went forward to be prayed for by her. I didn't have an expectation, but I was willing. She placed her hand on my head and said, "The lord says the last three chapters will be scrolls for Heaven". That day, I was preparing to write the last three chapters of my PhD. She stood back and asked me what I was doing. I told her, and she then prayed some more. That was all I needed. The courage to write and the motivation returned, and I began to write for a further year to develop a conceptual framework upon which strategies were developed which could improve care and support for children living as AIDS orphans in township communities. I am forever grateful for this time and the words spoken by Heidi. These scrolls were the development of a conceptual framework, the development of strategies, and key recommendations to policymakers concerning improving care and support for children living as AIDS orphans in township communities in South Africa.

I graduated, and the transition into academia began, but I will not write about this here. It's been a steep learning curve full of privilege and challenge. I've loved helping others attain undergraduate and postgraduate degrees. I've learned from my students and continue to learn from them. The Mamas and Mtutuzeli came to my PhD graduation. It was a great day for us all.

Mtutuzeli recently said, "I miss you here in South Africa, Sharron, but I am glad you aren't here somehow. I've had the space to lead and to become." I feel so proud of him and his wife. He is a man who visits widows and orphans living in Kwazakhele and surrounding township communities daily. Scripture says, "Pure religion is to visit widows and orphans" (James Chapter 1, v 27).

Chapter 12
Creating Hopeful Solutions
"Gold! gold! gold! gold! Bright and yellow, hard and cold!"
– Thomas Hood

Apart from being asked, "Why did you go to South Africa?", the next big question I am asked is, "Didn't you experience hopelessness whilst working in the townships?" The answer to that question is a resounding no. The resilience of children who became orphans is extraordinary. They uniquely developed resilience that needed to be supported and not undermined.

What seemed an overwhelming challenge to me was overshadowed by stories of endless hope and miraculous provision. As I listened to these children, I began to see their conversation surrounding the fact that I am, I can, I have. They had become orphans, but they were still their people: strong, clever, talented and willing to embrace the future. For example, "I am Sipo; I have a life and can go to school, and I will learn and be a good person." This strength was a resolve carved in a place of much adversity and loss.

A solution I created using the interviews I undertook with children as part of my master's degree was to develop guidelines for primary health care nurses working in clinics in township communities in South Africa. These guidelines centred around a planned care response to meet the unique needs of these children. This is about to be published in an academic journal (12).

My PhD centred on developing strategies to improve care and support for children living as AIDS orphans in township communities in South Africa. These strategies, which centre around four aspects that emerged during my PhD, will also be published in an academic journal (13).

1. Strengthening the legislative and policy framework of the South African government's response to children who have become AIDS orphans and who are living in township communities in South Africa. The legislative and policy framework is dense and comprehensive, but the pull-through to operationalisation is weak.

2. Enhancing the resilience of primary health care nurses, social workers, and psychologists through providing regular supervision for them.

3. Enabling interdisciplinary collaboration, bringing primary health care nurses, social workers, and psychologists together in a one-stop shop so that children can seek the professional assistance of these professionals at the same time in the same place. Like the Thutuzella "comfort centres" for women who have been sexually assaulted.

4. Facilitating an empowering work environment for these professionals to provide a space and resources to undertake support groups for these children (10, 11, 12, 13).

A note to policymakers, academics, church leaders and anyone who wants to help.

To the policymakers,

Thank you for all you have and do to support children living in township communities in South Africa. Your legislative and policy frameworks are rich but must be pulled through to be operationalised. There is an implementation gap. I leave you with this thought and ask you to re-read the Bill of Rights in your constitution. How can you begin to enable care and support for these vulnerable children? Every statement of intent that isn't operationalised to ensure children's "Best interests" are met increases their vulnerability. I leave you with the words of Nelson Mandela: "There is no keener revelation of the soul of a nation than how it cares for its children".

To academics,

Could we consider co-developing interventions across professional disciplines so these children can be cared for and more comprehensively supported?

A note to church leaders,

Could congregations be encouraged to visit widows and orphans regardless of the context? It is World Orphan's Day on the second Monday of November each year. Could events be held to raise money for NGOs who care for and support these vulnerable children? Could businessmen in congregations offer apprenticeship programs to assist these children in the workplace? Could celebration events be held on June 16 to mark South Africa's ratification of the Convention on Children's Rights? Could a National Day of Prayer be called to pray for children in South Africa?

To anyone who wants to help,

The GoGo Trust would welcome your support. You could host a fundraising event for us and would be welcome to accompany Mtutuzeli, Lungiswa, and me to Kwazakhele and surrounding township communities to visit our children and Mamas.

An African proverb says, "It takes a village to raise a child". You would be welcome to become part of our village.

Twenty per cent of the money raised through the sale of this book will go to the ongoing work of the GoGo Trust.

Conclusion

I Leave You With This

A Poem

What is hope? I mean real hope, the kind of hope that stirs your heart to faith and to praise. The kind of hope that makes you cry when you look in the face of it. The kind of hope that makes you jump high, sing without ceasing and cause you to embrace difficulty, mount the unmountable, think the unthinkable and do the undoable!!!! That kind of hope that stirs you amid darkness and causes you to sing like a Nightingale and dance like a ballerina. The kind of hope that makes your heart strong and weak all at the same time. The kind of hope that is full and tangible and the kind of hope that rescues you, refocuses you, and enables you to have a greater perspective. The kind of hope that draws one to the light makes you embrace a new day and sing a new song. The kind of hope that makes you love more extravagantly and live more victoriously – that kind of hope that causes a grown woman to dance in the rain. The kind of hope that causes you to be shipwrecked, persecuted, misunderstood, cast out, cast down, trampled on, and yet still sing a song to be heard above all sounds and cause those around to take notice because of the purity of its notes. It is a song so pure that the very notes of it create praise amid adversity, bringing glory to a good God from a place of poverty and pain. That can tell a story with the glance of an eye and reveal an actual character that can only be created by Jesus – the one who loves us completely.

I know that hope. I have seen that hope. I live that hope to see lives redeemed – the broken made whole. The sick healed, the downtrodden raised to new heights where the outside of the vessel is tarnished, broken, cast away and forgotten, and God has embraced the heart that has reached out to Him in brokenness and loss and created, just for Him, pure, beautiful, and undefiled praise. Where the circumstances are shocking, and the reality of poverty has broken the very essence of all the worth God gave when he made us in his image. In this, He created for himself something so beautiful, something so lovely, something so rich and enticing: He created hope for the hopeless, giving rise to extravagant praise – genuine praise not based on anything external but on the wealth given by a Savior to a failing heart. That kind of hope leaves one astounded and full of courage, the kind of hope that has embraced loss and is teaching a weak heart to trust in Him and His infinite goodness again. The kind of hope that takes a wounded heart and makes it sing again. The wonderful ability of a creator God to bring life and lay upon an orphan a crown of beauty instead of ashes, the oil of gladness instead of mourning, the garment of praise instead of a spirit of despair. Wow! What a wonderful Jesus. I know that hope. I have seen that hope. Only a Creator, loving God could reach into the heart of a broken child and enable them to see that they are perfectly loved. I know that God can do that. I have seen him do that. I see him do that all the time in the lives of our orphans and widows living in the township in South Africa. Watching a creative miracle bring life, hope, and love to adversity is a privilege.

– Sharron Frood, 2008

YELLOW, THE COLOUR OF HOPE

References

1. United Nations Committee on the Rights of the Child (CRC). (2016) UNICEF. Concluding observations on the second periodic report of South Africa 27 October 2016. URL:https://www.refworld.org/docid/5x87ce86b4.html.

2. Constitution of the Republic of South Africa. Act 108 of (1996). Pretoria, SA: Republic South Africa, URL: https://www.justice.gov.za/legislation/constitution/constitution-web-eng.pdf

3. Department of Women, Children and People with Disability. (2019) National Plan of Action for Children in South Africa Pretoria, SA: DWCPD. URL

4. Cutcliffe, J.R., McKenna, H.P.(2005) The Essential Concepts of Nursing. Elsevier, Churchill Livingstone.

5. Lansdown, G., & O'Kane, C. (2020) Child to Child Resource Centre Child to Child Approach.

6. Werner, D. (1993) Where there is no Doctor TALC.

7. Dickson. M (2021) Where there is no dentist, Hesperian Health Guides.

8. Frood S., Van Rooyen, R.M., & Ricks E, (2012) The experiences of children living as AIDS Orphans in Township Communities in South Africa (17) 10.4102/hsag.v17i1.568Health SA Gesondheid:

9. Mugumbate, J. R., Mupedziswa, R., Twikirize, J. M., Mthethwa, E., Desta, A. A., & Oyinlola, O. (2023) Understanding Ubuntu and its contribution to

social work education in Africa and other regions of the world. Social Work Education, 43(4), 1123–1139.https://doi.org/10.1080/02615479.2023.2168638.

10. Frood S., Van Rooyen, R.M., & Ricks E. (2018) Health and social care professionals' anguish in providing care and support to children who are AIDS orphans in Nelson Mandela Bay: A qualitative study. *IJANS,* 9(1)31-37.

11. Frood, S., & Purssell, E., (2020). "Barriers to" and "Recommendations for" providing care and support for children living as AIDS orphans in township communities in the Eastern Cape South Africa: A cluster analysis, International Journal of Africa Nursing Sciences, Volume 13, https://doi.org/10.1016/j.ijans.2020.100210.

12. Frood SL, Ricks E, Van Rooyen DM. (2023) The development of a conceptual framework for the "steps of progression strategies" to improve care and support to children who have become AIDS orphans and who are living in township communities in South Africa; Int J Child Health Hum Dev;16(1).

13. Frood, S.L., Ricks E., Van Rooyen, DM. (2023) Identifying and developing strategies to enable primary health care nurses, social workers, and psychologists to improve care and support for children who have become AIDS orphans living in township communities In South Africa Int J Child Health Hum Dev 2023;16(3):00-00.

SHARRON FROOD

About the Author

I grew up in Devon and moved to London to train as a nurse at Great Ormond Street Children's Hospital. After qualifying as a children's and adult nurse, I worked in paediatric neurology, neonatal Intensive care, paediatric surgery medicine and oncology.

Once qualified, I became a staff nurse at Great Ormond Street Hospital before attending bible school. I then spent time in Zambia, Uganda, and Tanzania. Following this, I earned a tropical nursing diploma from the London School of Hygiene and Tropical Medicine. After this, I volunteered at the House of Resurrection Haven in Port Elizabeth, South Africa, and the rest, I guess, is history.

After moving to Port Elizabeth (now known as Gqeberha), I began visiting widows and orphans living in Kwazakhele and surrounding township communities. During this time, I undertook an honours master's and PhD. The titles of these, respectively, are The Lived Experiences of Children Living as AIDS Orphans in Township Communities in South Africa and Identifying and Developing Strategies to Improve Care and Support to Children who have become AIDS Orphans and who are living in Township Communities in South Africa.

I founded the GoGo Trust in April 2003 and still oversee this work. I am currently working as an academic at a London University.

I have always loved the colour yellow and cheese.

Most importantly, the work of the GoGo Trust continues as you hold this book in your hand.

SHARRON FROOD

About the Organisation

We have just celebrated over 20 years of supporting widows and orphans in Kwazakhele and surrounding township communities in Gqeberha (formerly Port Elizabeth), South Africa.

www.gogotrust.org

About PublishU

PublishU is transforming the world of publishing.

PublishU has developed a new and unique approach to publishing books, offering a three-step guided journey to becoming a globally published author!

We enable hundreds of people a year to write their book within 100-days, publish their book in 100-days and launch their book over 100-days to impact tens of thousands of people worldwide.

The journey is transformative, one author said,

"I never thought I would be able to write a book, let alone in 100 days… now I'm asking myself what else have I told myself that can't be done that actually can?'"

To find out more visit

www.PublishU.com

SHARRON FROOD